CRACK: THE BROKEN PROMISE

Crack: 157592
The Broken Promise

DAVID F. ALLEN, M.D., M.P.H.
Lecturer in Public Health
Yale University School of Medicine

and

JAMES F. JEKEL, M.D., M.P.H.
Professor of Epidemiology and Public Health
Yale University School of Medicine

St. Martin's Press
New York

First published in the United States of America in 1991

Printed in Hong Kong

ISBN 0-312-05744-X

Library of Congress Cataloging-in-Publication Data

Allen, David Frankiin.
Crack: the broken promise / David F. Allen and James F. Jekel.
p.   cm.
Includes index.
ISBN 0-312-05744-X
1. Crack (Drug)   I. Jekel, James F.   II. Title
RC568.C6A55 1991
362.29'8 — dc20

90-25520
CIP

To our parents, who taught us to love what is good, and to our wives, who have surrounded us with love and goodness.

DFA & JFJ

Contents

Foreword

Cocaine is a chemical: a crystalline, odorless, colorless alkaloid, solid at room temperature. It is not a scourge or a demonic entity. Nor is it, itself, villainous, insidious, seductive or marvellous. It is not a salvation or a panacea. Of course, there are many claims that it is each of these. Cocaine easily passes from the blood into the brain. There it fits onto a specific few nerve cells in the brain in a way that amplifies the signals they transmit. Very unfortunately, those nerve cells regulate experiences of joy and pleasure, and the action of these cells, when first exposed to cocaine, is to produce intense feelings of well-being. We humans then assume a promise: that, when used again, and again, the cocaine crystals will have the same effect, and that if we use even more, the only result will be more pleasure. We thus extract a promise from cocaine, demanding that it continue to provide great joys, attained, in comparison to the normal pleasures in life, with astonishing ease. While the promise is alive, we call cocaine a euphoriant, an antidepressant, a therapeusis, and sometimes a salvation or a panacea. Because the brain adapts to external perturbations, including the presence of the cocaine crystals, the promise dies an inevitable death. Attempts to resurrect the promise destroys will and lives. We tend to blame the substance and neither the brain or ourselves, the extractors of the promise, and then label cocaine as villainous or seductive, as a demonic substance and scourge.

In *Crack: The Broken Promise* Allen and Jekel superbly explain the incomprehensible. How is it that crack cocaine can destroy judgement, will, and lives? And how is it that, sometimes, one can recover from this broken promise? It is difficult to find reasoned assessments of crack and even more rare to find clear descriptions of its effects – descriptions that neither distort, sensationalize, or misplace the key factors in cocaine addiction. The authors of *Crack: The Broken Promise* have been forced into reasoned assessments, and they ably share those assessments with us.

Dr Allen was the first to be faced with the spectre of 'crack' cocaine, which appeared first in the Bahamas almost a decade ago, and thus also the first treater faced with the need to respond to cries for help with crack addiction. His experience of almost a decade as the treatment leader in his nation's battle against 'crack' is unequalled. He has seen and treated all of the extremes of crack addiction. Dr Jekel has long experience in public health and its interactions with human behavior, and has been especially concerned with the human face of epidemics. He has catalogued the 'crack' epidemic from its origins in the Bahamas to its spread to the United States. Together, with the wisdom born of experience, they provide a complete view of crack, from the micromoment of a transient paranoid thought in a user to the behavior of nations over decades. Avoiding both oversimplification and unnecessary complication, they provide both the foundation and the details necessary for the concerned layman to understand and generate an informed response to 'crack' cocaine addiction.

Important questions face us about crack addiction. Will crack addiction spread? Where? How rapidly? In what communities? Will it pave the way for other drugs? Could other drugs be more powerful or more addictive? How did prior cocaine epidemics end? Will this one? How is this epidemic different? How does one act responsibly as a parent in an age of 'crack'? How does one identify early crack use? How does one intervene? How does crack work? How is crack different from other drugs? How and in what way does it change the addict? Does it change the brain or is it only a 'psychological' addiction? How often does recovery occur? In whom? What measures best help crack addicts? Which measures for which addicts? How long does it take recovery to occur? How potentially effective, or important, is prevention? What do the clinical effects of crack indicate for public policy decisions? What would be the consequences of legalization? How can we help and protect ourselves, our children, our friends, our communities, our countries? With clarity and essential brevity, Allen and Jekel provide the reader with the background to understand the complexities of these questions, to understand the answers that we have, and to understand the answers that we yet need.

FRANK GAWIN, MD
Director of Stimulant Abuse Treatment and Research
Yale University School of Medicine
April 1990

Preface

Our goal in this book is to provide health professionals and informed citizens throughout the world with a basic understanding of the world-wide epidemic of 'crack' cocaine abuse and an early warning of the kind of problem countries will probably face if they do not treat crack cocaine as the grave danger it is, and act accordingly. We discuss the disease, its history, treatment, and prevention, and some alternative strategies for control. We desire that other countries will take appropriate warning from what the Americas have suffered, in order to prevent a similar agony for themselves.

Many readers may suspect we exaggerate the dangers of freebase 'crack' cocaine. The Americas, however, ignored the warnings of many people (including ourselves) about the growing danger of crack cocaine until the crisis was upon them. The new dimensions of cocaine make it even more serious than during the first decade of this century, and many times as serious as cocaine seemed to be during the mid-1970s. If this book results in even a small increase in awareness and preparedness of individuals and nations for their struggle against crack cocaine, our efforts will have been well rewarded.

Ultimately the most important resource for resisting a widespread problem is the will and determination of the people, which requires that they understand the enemy, including how it threatens their most precious values and traditions. We hope this book will provide for its readers the basic information they need to understand and resist crack cocaine.

The discussion of the clinical aspects and treatment of crack abuse is intended to give readers enough information about signs and symptoms to detect crack abuse early in others and to assist effectively in the treatment of others, should that ever become necessary. Understanding the complexity of treatment also helps to clarify the true nature of cocaine abuse.

We also want this volume to provide basic information for policy makers unfamiliar with crack. We make no claim that this book is a complete information source for any group, but those who want more information can consult the various sources quoted here.

We are most grateful to our colleague, Frank Gawin, M.D., for his willingness to review the manuscript, make suggestions for improvement, and write the Foreword. His extensive knowledge and experience, and his special insight into the crack problem, improved the manuscript considerably. The responsibility for any errors and shortcomings, however, is ours alone.

With deepest gratitude we thank our wives, Vicki and Jan, for their unflagging support of this effort, despite the fact that for months it took much of the limited time we had 'just for them'. Beyond that, they were our editors, never failing to encourage us and yet never hesitating to tell us when a section needed rewriting. If this book is clear and informative to others, much of the credit belongs to them.

DAVID F. ALLEN
Nassau, Bahamas

JAMES F. JEKEL
New Haven, CT

May 1990

Introduction

A war threatens the normal existence of the Western Hemisphere, especially from Peru to the United States and Canada. The enemy in the war is freebase ('crack') cocaine and the forces promoting the drug, who are so ruthless and powerful as to make the Sicilian Mafia appear gentle and weak by comparison.

Britain and Europe currently have major illicit drug activity, including heroin, methamphetamine ('speed'), and powdered cocaine hydrochloride, but so far they have largely escaped the 'blitzkrieg' of crack cocaine. Their grace period, however, is near an end. Britain and Europe are the next major target for invasion by the cocaine cartels. *Newsweek* magazine reported that 29 times the amount of cocaine was seized in Europe in 1988 as in 1980.[1]

The drug forces have been spectacularly successful in the Western Hemisphere because, despite early warnings, none of the involved nations took the threat of crack cocaine seriously until it was well established.

Crack cocaine is a great unmasker of a society's values. It quickly strips away the pretenses of a culture. If pleasure and quick profit are the leading values, cocaine will soon fill that nation with addiction and corruption. Over the last two decades, cocaine has increased from a relatively small business to an estimated trade of almost $150 billion *per year*. This could only happen if crack cocaine itself had an appeal. It does. It promises a lot: if taken in the prescribed way, crack provides one of the most intense forms of pleasure known to man. But this promise is insidiously broken, as it thrusts the user into addiction, crime, misery, and degradation. This book is about the broken promise of crack.

As a further concern, clouds are gathering on the horizon in the form of crystalline methamphetamine ('ice'), which appears to be starting to hit the West like a second wave of crack, and for the invasion of which crack paves the way. Methamphetamine, like crack, is a brain stimulant, is commonly known as 'speed' and is found throughout Britain and Europe. 'Ice' is a smokable form of 'speed', so that it is to ordinary speed what crack is to powdered cocaine. The more rapid form of delivery gives it a much more rapid

1

and concentrated (and therefore powerful) effect, both in producing good feelings (euphoria) and subsequent bad feelings (dysphoria). To date, however, the spread of 'ice' has been limited mostly to Hawaii and the Western US. If crack cocaine paves the way for 'ice', there is a double urgency to the crack problem.

A BRIEF HISTORY OF COCAINE

Cocaine was not always the problem it is now and many are surprised to learn that Britain and Europe, as well as the United States of America, have lived through a previous cocaine epidemic. The history of cocaine is important in order to understand why we are now in the midst of a major world-wide increase in cocaine abuse. Cocaine is derived from the plant *Erythroxylon coca* which grows best above 1000 feet elevation on the Western slopes of the Andes mountains. For centuries its leaves have been chewed in Peru, Bolivia, Chile, and Colombia for its stimulant effect. It is believed that coca leaf chewing goes back long before the Inca Empire was established.[2] The Incas viewed the plant as of divine origin, from the god Inti, to relieve hunger, thirst, and ease the burden of life. Another myth holds that the coca plant was sent as a curse by a woman, in order to punish her captors, who executed her for adultery.

In the Inca civilization, the use of the coca leaf was well regulated. It was used mainly for ceremonial occasions or to reward soldiers or others for outstanding accomplishments. The ritualistic use of coca leaves required that they be chewed into a ball and then an alkaline substance called 'tocra' was added to release the cocaine from the organic material of the leaf. Chewing the leaf provided a long-lasting, low grade euphoria, which reduced appetite and increased physical stamina. However, strict controls over the use of coca leaf minimized its negative consequences for the Indians.[3] This regulation of coca leaf chewing continued until the 1500s, when the Incas were eventually conquered by Pizarro.

After the arrival of the Spaniards, coca leaf chewing became widespread. Initially the Church forbade the Indians to chew coca leaves, but then it was discovered that coca leaf chewing enabled the Indians to work harder on less food in the high altitudes. King Phillip I of Spain then issued an imperial decree that coca leaf chewing was necessary for the well being of the Indians. Thus cocaine was used to enable the Indians to be exploited – to work longer and harder for less pay. This is an early illustration of how cocaine tends to make people put economic issues above moral concerns. Even today, chewing coca leaves remains a disruptive force in some areas of South America, where people are often paid in coca leaves rather than in money.[4]

COCAINE IN EUROPE

Coca leaves were transported to Europe from the 17th century on by Spanish explorers, but it was not until 1859 that Albert Niemann of the University of Gottigen in Germany synthesized cocaine hydrochloride powder. In the same year, the Italian neurologist Pablo Mantegazza wrote his prize-winning essay praising cocaine's ability to reduce fatigue, increase strength, raise spirits, and increase sexual potency.[5]

In 1863, Angelo Mariani combined cocaine with wine to create *Vin Mariani* which was promoted widely and was used by such notables as Robert Lewis Stevenson and Henrick Ibsen. Mariani was given a gold medal and cited as a benefactor of humanity by Pope Leo XIII, a frequent user of the drink.

In 1880 a Russian nobleman, Professor Vassili von Anrep, discovered the local anesthetic properties of cocaine on mucous membranes, and in 1884, Sigmund Freud, a student of Professor von Anrep, experimented with ingesting cocaine powder and described it as a wonder drug that 'lifts the spirit, decreases fatigue, relieves impotence, and cures depression'.[6] Freud used cocaine to treat his friend von Fleishel for morphine addiction, but von Fleishel became addicted to the cocaine and developed a cocaine psychosis, during which he was delirious and saw snakes crawling over himself.

In 1885 Albrecht Erlenmeyer accused Freud of unleashing cocaine as the third scourge of humanity, after alcohol and opiates. As more of his patients became addicted, Freud turned from promoting to opposing cocaine.

 ## COCAINE IN NORTH AMERICA

The popularity of cocaine as a local anaesthetic, as well as a possible treatment for narcotic addiction, spread quickly among professionals in the United States. A number of scientists, including Dr.

William Halsted, experimented with cocaine to validate the claims made about the drug. Halsted, a noted surgeon from Johns Hopkins University, became addicted by snorting cocaine, resulting in the ruin of his life and practice. Wishing to help him, his friends sent him on a trip around the world, hoping he would forget cocaine, or at least lose his appetite for it. However, upon returning, Halsted, although he no longer used cocaine, struggled with morphine abuse for the remainder of his life.[7]

In 1885, John Styth Pemberton of Georgia introduced French wine 'Cola' to compete with 'Vin Mariani', and sold his 'Cola' as the ideal nerve and tonic stimulant. In 1886, he developed Coca-Cola, a popular soft drink made from a syrup of coca and caffeine. Cocaine was further popularized when Dr. W. A. Hammond, a leader of the American medical profession, endorsed the virtues of cocaine use. As a result, persons in lower socioeconomic groups, particularly in dry states, increasingly started using cocaine instead of hard liquor.

Meanwhile, the medical profession became more aware of the problems of cocaine abuse and of its failure to cure opiate and alcohol addictions. In fact, in 1891, 200 cases of death by cocaine intoxication were reported.

A belief developed, particularly in the south-eastern United States, that black persons acquired extraordinary powers through using cocaine, giving them the ability to defy laws and commit violent crimes. In 1903, cocaine was removed from Coca-Cola because of the fears of southern politicians about cocaine's effect on black persons. One of the strongest motivations for making cocaine illegal in the United States was the general perception that cocaine increased the risk of crime among blacks, especially the crime of rape.[8]

However, importation of coca increased, and it is estimated that Americans consumed as much cocaine in 1906 as they did in 1976, with only half the population. In 1906, the increasing fear of addiction and crime from drugs was one of the motivations for passing the Food and Drug Act. This Act required, among other things, the elimination of cocaine from patent medicines and soft drinks and heralded the beginning of the end of the free and easy distribution of cocaine.

With unemployment rising, cocaine use in the USA peaked in 1907, when an estimated 1.5 million pounds of cocaine entered the country. The situation was especially acute in New York, and this led to the passage of the New York Anti-Cocaine Bill, which clamped down hard on the widespread use of cocaine. In 1908, importation of coca leaves had dropped to half of the level of the previous year, and public pressures were increasing against cocaine users. Indeed, addicts were considered to be 'cocaine fiends' who should be allowed to die. Although cocaine use did decline in the general population, its popularity among intellectuals and writers increased, probably due to its reputation for stimulating creativity.

By 1914, forty-six states had passed laws regulating the use and distribution of cocaine. This set the pace for the passage of the Harrison Narcotics Act, which provided for a complete ban on cocaine, although it was incorrectly classified as a narcotic in the Act. With the passage of this act, cocaine became less available, and its price subsequently increased. The Act was amended in 1919, placing even stricter controls on cocaine and opium, whereupon cocaine became more scarce and its price rose to approximately $30 per ounce, three times as high as a decade earlier. Prohibitively expensive, cocaine use became restricted to the bohemian–jazz culture and the ghetto, where it was a symbol of affluence.

Clearly, cocaine abuse is not a new problem in the West. However, with the advent of crack, the form and power of its abuse is new, and these changes are responsible for the appearance of the spreading world-wide epidemic (often called a 'pandemic') of cocaine abuse. The US National Drug Control Strategy put it this way:

What, then, accounts for the intensifying drug-related chaos that we see every day in our newspapers and on television? One word explains much of it. That word is *crack*.[9]

The reasons why the crack problem has appeared now will be discussed in Chapter 1.

References

1. C. Dickey, 'A Common Market of Crack?', *Newsweek*, 18 Sept. 1989.
2. E. Van Dyke, and R. Byck, 'Cocaine', *Scientific American* 246: 128–46, 1982.

3.   R. Ashley, *Cocaine: Its History and Effects* (New York: St. Martin's Press, 1975).
4.   R. Jeri, Personal Communication.
5.   G. Austin, 'Cocaine USA', in *Perspectives on the History of Psychoactive Substance Use* (Rockville, MD: National Institute on Drug Abuse Research Monograph No. 24, 1978).
6.   S. Freud, 'Uber Coca', in R. Byck, *Cocaine Papers* (New York: Stonehill Publishing, 1974), pp. 49–73.
7.   L. Grinspoon, and J. B. Bakalar, *Cocaine: A Drug and its Social Evolution*, (Revised Edition) (New York: Basic Books, 1985), p. 31.
8.   D. Musto, *The American Disease: Origins of Narcotic Control*, Expanded Edition (New York: Oxford University Press, 1987).
9.   The White House, *National Drug Control Strategy*, September 1989, p. 3.

1 The Crack Crisis

WHY NOW?

Many parts of the world face a major crisis due to crack cocaine. Neighborhoods and cities are now being overwhelmed with crack-related problems, such as: addicted men, women, and children; destruction of families; increased crime; stressed medical care facilities; overburdened police forces, courts, and prisons; and loss of productivity. But why now? What has happened to bring this problem to the fore at this moment in history? A fundamental purpose of this chapter, indeed of this book, is to explain why some nations are now inundated by, and all nations are threatened by, a new form of cocaine, despite the fact that until recently cocaine was thought by most people to be relatively harmless.

One other period of history, from about 1885 to 1930, was marked by a major cocaine problem in Europe and America. In Europe the problem was partly stimulated by Sigmund Freud, who at first considered cocaine to be safe.[1] In the US those who used cocaine eventually were called 'cocaine fiends', and even a movie by this title was made, which was largely a propaganda film against the drug.[2] Cocaine appeared in songs, such as one that began 'Cocaine Bill and Morphine Sue . . . '. Both continents went through a cycle that began with a belief in cocaine's innocence (or even benefit), from about 1885 to about 1900. This progressed to growing dismay and intolerance (from perhaps 1900 until World War I), and then major opposition, including laws with enforcement, from the end of World War I to about 1930, by which time the use of cocaine became extremely limited.

A central question is whether or not the current crack epidemic will go through similar historical phases of innocence, awakening, general resistance, and resolution that characterized the cocaine epidemic in the first two decades of this century. Can we assume that with the passage of time an effective general opposition and resistance to crack addiction will develop in society, as happened earlier against snorted cocaine, thus enabling it to be controlled? If so it may be wise to try to hasten this process, but in doing so we should be careful not to damage our freedoms, discriminate

7

against population groups heavily involved, or de-rail the historical processes.

On the other hand, if the modern crack epidemic and the current world situation differ in a major way from that in the early part of this century, we cannot assume some vague historical processes will accomplish the difficult task of conquering the crack problem. One of the world's leading historians of addictive diseases, David Musto, believes that during the last 15 years society has been going through similar phases with regard to cocaine as in the early part of the century: first a belief that cocaine was a harmless recreational drug; second, developing awareness of its dangers; and third, growing opposition to it.[3] Back then, the use of the drug spread from the wealthier classes to the poor, as it has in the US over the past 15 years or so. Also during the first cocaine epidemic in the USA, revulsion to the drug, based on awareness of its dangers, began in the more educated groups and spread to the the poor. Since the mid-1980s, awareness of many of the dangers of cocaine, especially crack, has rapidly increased in the more educated groups in the USA, with some apparent effects. The number of first time users among high schools students has dropped, and there may even have been a small drop in cocaine-related deaths and medical emergencies.[4] Whether or not the peak incidence of new users in the US has passed is uncertain, but the peak incidence of problems among those who *already* have become crack addicts in the 1980s is still to be faced, and the epidemic rages largely unchecked in the poorer areas of most large cities in the US, as well as in many other countries.[5]

We believe that the current crack epidemic is different in important ways from the cocaine problem in the early part of the century, both because crack is more rapidly addictive than powdered cocaine, and because Western society is quite different in its culture, commerce, values, and attitudes toward the use of substances that produce a psychic effect. We doubt that anyone can make confident assumptions about the future course of the present crack problem, based either on the historical cocaine problem or on the behavior of other epidemic diseases. Even if we could assume that the current problem would eventually disappear of its own accord, nations will not be able to tolerate the social and economic damage that would result between now and the time when the historical process would eventually bring crack under control.

Musto correctly suggests that one reason cocaine has become a major problem for the second time in this century is the long delay (years) from when a population begins to use snorted or ingested cocaine until the onset of large scale addiction.[6] The current crack epidemic, which began in the US in the mid-1980s, was preceded in the 1970s by widespread use of diluted powdered cocaine by intranasal snorting. In that decade powdered cocaine again began to appear in abundant quantities at middle class parties. There the cocaine powder (hydrochloride) was snorted into the nose through a straw or rolled-up currency bill. Recreational snorting of cocaine powder, if the powder is diluted ('cut'), may not be rapidly addicting for most persons, so that many people, especially those who did recreational snorting in the 1970s, came to believe cocaine was a relatively harmless recreational drug. Had crack cocaine been available and widely used in the 1970s, the delay between the start of cocaine use and the appearance of an epidemic would have been much shorter.

The groundwork for a tolerant attitude toward cocaine in the 1970s was prepared for by the 1960s, which ushered in a new era of drug experimentation and toleration, especially with hallucinogens such as LSD and marijuana ('pot'). In the early and middle 1970s, the greatest societal concern regarding *stimulants* was directed at methamphetamine ('speed') rather than against cocaine powder. It was common to see the slogan 'Speed Kills' on bumper stickers, although many older Americans probably thought the slogan referred to highway velocity. 'Speed', like cocaine, is a stimulant (an 'upper', to use the street term). It produces pleasant feelings by a mechanism similar to that of cocaine. Also in the 1970s there was an increase in the use of sedatives ('downers') for their psychic effect. One of the most common of these was methaqualone ('Quaaludes'). There was international debate concerning whether or not all of these drugs were safe, although most of them remained illegal in the US, except for medically prescribed therapeutic or research uses.

Throughout these decades there also was a steady, if subdued, concern about the most important of the intravenous drugs, heroin, which is related to opium and morphine. Efforts to provide methadone maintenance and other treatments for heroin use continued, but drug treatment was not seen as medically glamorous or of the highest importance. This was partly because in the US heroin was largely confined to a less visible population of inner-city poor persons who formed a kind of underclass, and because its use was not increasing at a rate that suggested an epidemic or a major threat to middle America.

These attitudes continued until the discovery of Acquired Immune Deficiency Syndrome (AIDS) in 1981 and the subsequent clarification of the role of intravenous drug use in its spread. Even now, the increasing attention being paid to intravenous heroin use is more because of its potential to spread AIDS than because of the direct effects of the heroin.

In the 1970s, although cocaine was illegal except for medical use, there was relatively little concern about its safety on the part of the medical profession as well as the population at large. In fact, a respected textbook of psychiatry[7] asserted in 1980 that '. . . taken no more than two or three times per week, cocaine creates no serious problems'. Also, the American Psychiatric Association's official manual of psychiatric diagnosis (DSM–III) did not even have a category for cocaine dependence, because the drug was not thought to produce a substance abuse problem.[8] In 1974 a drug expert wrote,

> Cocaine . . . is probably the most benign of illicit drugs currently in widespread use. At least as strong a case could be made for legalizing it as for legalizing marijuana. Short acting – about 15 minutes – not physically addicting, and acutely pleasurable, cocaine has found increasing favor at all socioeconomic levels in the last year.[9]

Musto argues that this lax attitude toward cocaine reflected lack of knowledge of the seriousness of the first epidemic of cocaine.[10] Surprisingly, however, the authors of the textbook chapter quoted above, Grinspoon and Bakalar, also wrote a book entitled *Cocaine: A Drug and Its Social Evolution* published in 1976, which contained much history about cocaine.[11] These authors, as well as most drug specialists, not only did not anticipate the crack epidemic, but they even missed the threat that powdered cocaine presented, probably in part because they lacked the actual experience of the previous cocaine epidemic.

Another reason for the lack of concern about the cocaine snorting of the middle and late 1970s was that there had not been enough lead time for significant numbers of cocaine snorters to become addicted and appear in treatment facilities.[12] The major cause of the present problem, however, was the appearance in the early 1980s of ready-to-smoke freebase cocaine (crack), which was more addictive and dangerous than the earlier dilute cocaine powder by an order of magnitude. The cocaine snorting of the 1970s may have started out to be similar to the wave of cocaine at the turn of the century, but what has happened in the 1980s has been quite different in its explosiveness, and even an intimate knowledge of cocaine's history in the US and Europe would not have fully prepared one for what has happened in the past decade.

The medical literature no longer hesitates to proclaim the danger of cocaine use, especially of smoking crack. In 1985 Grinspoon and Bakalar felt compelled to write a revised edition of their book, explaining their reasons in the Preface:

> The most important development is that cocaine use and abuse have spread much more widely than was anticipated by us and by most other researchers studying the question in 1976. Cocaine has become a greater social problem than at any time in its previous history . . . [13]

If the appearance of crack cocaine is the central reason our present drug problem appeared when it did, a second reason is the fact that early in the 1980s it was discovered how crack could be made easily and safely from powdered cocaine (which is the form of cocaine use for smuggling) in any kitchen. Third, the use of modern marketing methods by the cocaine dealers has helped to speed up the spread of crack in the western hemisphere.

A BRIEF CHRONOLOGY OF THE CURRENT EPIDEMIC

Storm Warnings

The earliest warnings of a new epidemic of crack abuse came from South America, around 1972, particularly from the writings of Jeri.[14-15] He documented an urban pattern of cocaine abuse in Peru in which the users smoked a cheap and impure form of cocaine known as *coca paste*, usually after putting it in regular or marijuana cigarettes. The smokers rapidly became so totally involved in cocaine use that nothing else mattered to them. This form of total immersion in cocaine led to poverty, illegal acts to obtain money for the drug, malnutrition and rapidly developing ill health, and even to death.[16] Coca paste is an impure intermediate product of the production of cocaine hydrochloride powder, and consists of a varying mixture of cocaine sulphate, cocaine phosphate, cocaine freebase, methanol, kerosene, sulphuric acid, and other substances. It is not surprising that smoking coca paste was found to be devastating to the lungs of smokers, in addition to the other harm it produced.

Jeri's papers, however, were not well known to English-speaking scientists, because they were mostly written in Spanish, and even scientists from the northern hemisphere who became familiar with what was happening in South America did not anticipate that a similar scenario soon would appear in North America or Europe.

In 1980, comedian Richard Pryor accidentally received serious burns, allegedly when the ether he was using to prepare crack from cocaine powder ignited. At that time, most of the world did not know what he was preparing or why.

In 1982, the comedian John Belushi died from a 'speedball' injected by a female friend in a Los Angeles hotel room. A speedball is a combination of a stimulant and an opiate taken at the same time, under the shaky theory that each drug tends to counteract the side effects of the other. Usually, as in Belushi's case, the speedball is a combination of heroin (a depressant) and cocaine (a stimulant) dissolved in water and injected intravenously. Also by 1982, clinics and emergency rooms had begun to see cocaine abusers in some quantity.[17]

In May 1983 the first US cocaine hotline, 1–800–COCAINE, started for the purpose of obtaining epidemiologic and clinical data, while at the same time assisting the callers with education, counselling, and referrals.[18] The first survey of hotline callers, in 1983, found that most abusers who called were well educated, had an adequate income, and had been using the drug for about 5 years. At that time, the average user was spending $640 per *week* on cocaine. Within 3 months of its beginning, the hotline had to expand to 24 hour service and add lines to handle the increased volume of calls. The next survey, two years later, showed that more cocaine users were using crack, and, on the average, they were not as wealthy or as well educated. By 1988, the hotline had responded to more than two million calls.

Beginning in 1983, a sudden appearance of large numbers of crack abusers in the Bahamas overwhelmed the existing treatment capabilities of that country; this was to become the first documented nationwide epidemic of freebase cocaine (crack) abuse outside of a producer nation.[19] In the initial medical report from the Bahamas, the authors warned that the Bahamian experience might soon be reflected in other Western nations. In numerous speaking engagements and discussions with medical colleagues in 1985 and 1986, we predicted that the cocaine problem would expand greatly and might even rival Acquired Immune Deficiency Syndrome (AIDS) as a societal concern in the West. Those suggestions, however, were usually met with disbelief. Again, why this doubt as recently as 1986? One reason seemed to be the fact that the West had been using cocaine fairly heavily for 10 years or so, and few citizens or physicians had yet seen persons with cocaine abuse, although they were being seen in increasing quantity by psychiatrists and emergency rooms.

A Hurricane

The latter half of the 1980s have seen the full fury of crack abuse unleashed on the Americas, and growing hints of its harmful potential have been seen in other areas of the world, including Western Europe. Crack is an egalitarian drug: every race and socioeconomic class in the Americas has been heavily impacted by it.

Originally, cocaine snorting was mostly a habit of the upper or middle classes, partly due to the high cost of the drug. In the 1980s, however, the drop in the price of cocaine, and a major switch to smoking crack, opened its use to all classes. Since then, increasingly it has become a scourge of lower income groups in central cities. For example, the lead article in the August 11, 1989, *New York Times* stated:

> Crack is rapidly accelerating the destruction of families in poor urban neighborhoods where mothers are becoming increasingly addicted and children are selling the drug in greater numbers than ever before.[20]

Some of the evidence for this statement included the fact that in high crack use areas, more and more children were taking over as the family head, because from selling crack they earned most of the family income. It has been reported that teenage girls are leaving their families to form gangs to sell or buy crack.[21]

Children's involvement in the crack trade may initially be tolerated by the family, because the children bring home money and gifts that the parent or parents need and want. When the dangers of this lifestyle become clear, it is usually too late to influence it. In fact, if the cocaine trade invades a neighborhood in a major way, it is difficult for parents to control the problem. Women are almost as likely as men to use crack. Female crack abusers may indulge in prostitution in order to obtain money for the drug, which brings a risk of acquiring and spreading AIDS. If they become pregnant, female crack users deliver babies with severe and probably permanent damage to the nervous systems. Female heads of households, who traditionally have been the ones who held poor families together, are increasingly themselves becoming crack addicts, resulting in complete family disintegration.

The US statistics of crime and violence are growing at an alarming rate, and much of the increase is blamed mostly on crack;[22] recent surveys of voter concerns, including the 1989 Gallup Poll of US citizens, put drug abuse at or near the top of the list.[23] Another disturbing but consistent pattern in the US is that although the cocaine problem is most severe in the poorer areas of major cities, cocaine trafficking now operates in small towns and rural areas as well.[24-27] Suburban cocaine users tend to obtain their drug in the inner cities, although they may use it elsewhere. The usual pattern is for drug forces to establish themselves in large cities and then, when well entrenched, to begin a centrifugal spread outward to the suburbs and rural towns from their urban bases.

A Confluence of Forces

As was implied above, several forces have converged in the 1980s to make cocaine a national and international disaster in the making: a switch from snorted to inhaled (crack) cocaine; a technical advance in crack manufacture; a major increase in cocaine production; and increasingly sophisticated methods of drug smuggling and marketing.[28]

Freebase (crack) cocaine
To understand the central role of freebase cocaine in the current situation, some elementary facts are needed about the effects of cocaine on the brain. The euphoria (good feelings) produced by cocaine are in *direct proportion to the rapidity with which the blood*

level of cocaine rises, rather than to the ultimate blood level achieved. The South American custom of *chewing coca leaf* produces a slow release of fairly small quantities of cocaine, and the blood level rises only slowly. Therefore, the effect of chewing coca leaf, though pleasurable, is mild and is seldom dangerous or addictive.

The habit of *snorting powdered cocaine hydrochloride into the nose* through a straw produces a much faster rise in the blood level, beginning in 5–15 minutes with a peak at 15–30 minutes. The faster rise in blood cocaine level produces a much greater euphoria than does chewing coca leaf, but the euphoria is of shorter duration. Also, when the usual amounts of cocaine snorted in the 1970s was spread over the few square inches of the mucous membrane on the inside of the nose by snorting, absorption was relatively slow. Moreover, cocaine reduces the blood flow to the membranes of the nose and thereby slows the rate of absorption of the cocaine. For all of these reasons, the cocaine snorted recreationally in the 1970s usually produced only a moderate level of euphoria and a moderate risk of addiction and medical problems. Even snorting of cocaine produces many addicted individuals, however, and it should never be considered safe.

Both inhaling crack cocaine and injecting dissolved cocaine hydrochloride powder give an extremely rapid rise in the blood level of cocaine. In fact, a sudden pleasurable effect (the 'hit') is felt in 8–12 seconds from starting to inhale or inject, and the euphoria is far more intense than by other methods. The high lasts only a short time, about 5–15 minutes.

One might wonder why inhaling crack cocaine would produce such a rapid high, particularly when it is not as soluble on moist surfaces as the hydrochloride powder. The reason is that the lungs of a normal person have approximately the surface area of a tennis court, so that all of the crack vapor has almost immediate contact with a large absorptive surface. Both inhaling and injecting cocaine produce similar effects, but inhaling is easier and does not involve the dangers of intravenous injection, so it is growing in popularity faster than injection and in groups that might not consider intravenous drug use. The greater the degree of euphoria (the 'high'), the greater is the degree of dysphoria (the 'low') which follows, and these two factors largely determine the addictive potential of the drug.

The dysphoria which follows cessation of crack use can be severe, including depression, sleep disturbances, and fatigue. During this period, the only thing that can be counted on to relieve the depression and other symptoms of cocaine withdrawal is more cocaine. Thus the drug becomes self-reinforcing, with both a 'pull' (to obtain more pleasure) and a 'push' (to relieve the unpleasant after effects).

Thus the first element in the new cocaine picture of the 1980s is what amounts to a new drug: freebase (crack) cocaine. Prior to this decade, only a few intravenous drug users knew about intravenous cocaine, and few Americans were interested in becoming involved with intravenous drug use. Smoking has been the favorite American way of taking in legal drugs (nicotine in cigarettes) or illegal drugs (e.g., marijuana), and smoking has been associated with safety in the eyes of the population. The smoking of crack, however, provided a more rapid, less costly, and, initially, an *apparently* safer way to get an extreme high from cocaine than did any other method (the apparent safety partly involved not having to use intravenous injection to get the rapid high). This new form of cocaine, crack, is a critical reason the current epidemic differs in important ways from the past.

Technologic 'advances' in cocaine manufacture
Crack would not have become as widely available had it not been for the discovery of a new, cheap, and safe way to make crack from the cocaine hydrochloride powder. This new manufacturing method, which uses sodium bicarbonate and water, allowed anybody to make freebase cocaine. Consequently this new technique *decentralized* the production of freebase cocaine to the most basic level – the pusher and even the consumer. No longer did one have to risk self-immolation from ether (as did Richard Pryor) to make crack cocaine. The crackling sound produced by the chemical reactions of the sodium bicarbonate method of freebase cocaine production, and also when it is smoked, apparently led to the street name 'crack'. Thus, by the early 1980s, crack – which is addictive enough that it could increase its own demand by astronomical proportions – also could be made safely almost anywhere.

Increased cocaine production
Along with the new forms of cocaine delivery and the increasing numbers of addicts came increased demand. The cocaine producers in South America – particularly those in Colombia, which is the South American centre for manufacture and shipment of cocaine – have steadily increased the supply since the late 1970s.

The resulting drop in price helped to fuel the new demand for more of the drug, and a cycle of increased demand and production was begun.

Improved marketing methods

One reason the use of crack is spreading so fast is that modern marketing methods have been used more than for any previous illicit drug.[29] The coordinated switch by pushers in the Bahamas to selling only the crack form of cocaine was, in effect, a marketing trial that was a huge success from the pusher's viewpoint, and it was was soon copied elsewhere.

One of the principles of modern marketing is to develop products for increasingly small market segments at prices each segment can afford. Crack pushers accomplished this by creating prepackaged units at more-or-less standard sizes and prices. This was done by selling standard sized plastic vials containing $5, $10, or $20 of crack cocaine in each. Pushers began offering rebates (usually 10 per cent back) when the plastic vials used to package the crack were returned. The rebates helped to bring the users back to the pushers, and the rebate was usually taken in more of the drug. This marketing ploy also helped to solve a supply problem for the pushers: obtaining enough plastic vials had become difficult, and return of the vials helped to maintain their supply.[30] Crack increases its own on-the-street sales force because many addicts find they must become pushers in order to make enough money to sustain their own habits. Also they can get cocaine powder at 'wholesale' prices this way and make their own crack. In most cities, young boys become 'hawkers', who make the street sales, often to people in cars, and then run into a building or to a special nearby car to obtain the product after taking the order. This is a modern version of the 'car hop'! It has even been reported that in one area, crack was distributed from a neighborhood ice cream truck.

Another marketing method is the 'base house', a fortified and guarded house where users can buy crack, have comradeship and protection, and even, if desired, order other drugs and/or prostitutes. If police approach, the lookouts give enough warning for drugs to be flushed down a toilet, and what remains usually is not enough to interest a prosecutor.[31] A communal approach to drug use is not new. Opium smoking was often done in 'opium dens', and intravenous drug users frequently prefer injecting in communal settings popularly known as 'shooting galleries'. However, the base houses appear to be new in that protection by armed guards is provided, and a variety of drugs are available. Base houses are becoming 'supermarkets' of illegal pleasures.

Still another new element in the Western drug scene is experimentation with drug mixtures. One recently reported mixture is cocaine and phencyclidine (PCP, 'Angel Dust'), which is called 'space basing'.[32] This apparently produces wild behavior and paranoia.

PATTERNS OF SPREAD OF DRUG USE

Cocaine use, including crack, has followed a similar pattern to that of many drugs. Discovery and use started with experimentation in special population groups, such as the wealthy and bohemian/artist groups. It then was used as a recreational drug by the middle class, which eventually realized the dangers of the drug and began to control its use. From there, use of the drug proceeds down through the social strata of society until it reaches the lowest socioeconomic groups, where it becomes a devastating and persistent problem.[33]

This is not to say that the crack problem has disappeared from the middle classes. However, a 1989 household drug use survey estimated that the percentage of persons in the US using any illegal drug within the preceding 30 days had dropped since 1985 from 23 million to 14.5 million, and that the use of marijuana was down 36 per cent and cocaine use was down 48 per cent.[34] This must be interpreted with caution, as many other measures show problems from crack use to be increasing. But it does suggest that the existence of a serious drug problem has begun to impact upon the attitudes and behaviors of many Americans who previously felt comfortable with illegal drugs. This may form the basis of stronger national resistance against drug use, but in the meantime, millions of persons are addicted to drugs, particularly to crack. In a poem undoubtedly referring to other experiences, but which describes with uncanny accuracy the experiences of crack abuse, the American poet, Emily Dickinson, who lived from 1830 to 1886, wrote:

> For each ecstatic instant
> We must an anguish pay
> In keen and quivering ratio
> To the ecstasy.

For each beloved hour
Sharp pittances of years
Bitter contested farthings
And coffers heaped with tears.[35]

References

1. D. F. Musto, *The American Disease: Origins of Narcotic Control (Expanded Edition)* (New York: Oxford Univ. Press, 1973), p. 7; and M. Wortman 'Behind the Drug-War Lines', *Yale Magazine*, Nov. 1989, pp. 42–7.
2. 'The Cocaine Fiends', directed by C. A. O'Connor, 1936.
3. Musto, op. cit.
4. *New York Times* 'Health Chief Tells of a Decrease in the Number of Cocaine Addicts', 15 May 1990; and *New Haven Register*, 'Drug Deaths Are Dropping', 24 May 1990.
5. US News & World Report, 'The streets are filled with coke', 5 March 1990, p. 24.
6. Musto, op. cit.
7. L. Grinspoon and J. B. Bakalar, 'Drug Dependence: Non-narcotic Agents', in *Comprehensive Textbook of Psychiatry*, 3rd Edition, edited by H. I. Kaplan, A. M. Freedman, and B. J. Sadock (Baltimore: Williams and Wilkins, 1980).
8. F. H. Gawin and H. D. Kleber, 'Evolving Conceptualizations of Cocaine Dependence', *Yale Journal of Biological Medicine* 61: 123–36 (1988).
9. P. G. Bourne, 'The Great Cocaine Myth', *Drugs and Drug Abuse Education Newsletter* 5:5 (1974) (as quoted in D. F. Musto, op. cit., p. 265).
10. Musto, op. cit.
11. L. Grinspoon and J. B. Bakalar, *Cocaine: A Drug and Its Social Evolution* (Revised Edition) (New York: Basic Books, 1985).
12. Gawin and Kleber, op. cit.
13. Grinspoon and Bakalar, op. cit.
14. F. R. Jeri *et al.*, 'Consumo de Drogas Peligrosas por Miembros y Familiares de la Fuerza Armada y Fuerzo Policial Peruana', *Revista de la Sanidad de las Fuerzas Policiales* 37:104–12 (1976).
15. F. R. Jeri *et al.*, 'El Sindrome de la Pasta de Coca: Observaciones en un Grupo de 158 Pacientes del Area de Lima', *Revista de la Sanidad del Ministerio del Interior* 39:1–18 (1978).
16. F. R. Jeri, 'Coca-paste Smoking in Some Latin American Countries: A Severe and Unabated Form of Addiction', *Bulletin on Narcotics* 36(2): 15–31 (1984).

20 *Crack: The Broken Promise*

17. Gawin and Kleber, op. cit.
18. H. Roehrich and M. S. Gold, '800-COCAINE: Origins, Significance, and Findings', *Yale Journal of Biology and Medicine* 61: 149–55 (1988).
19. J. F. Jekel, D. Allen *et al.*, 'Epidemic Cocaine Abuse: A Case Study from the Bahamas', *The Lancet* i: 459–62, 1986.
20. G. Kolata, 'In Cities, Poor Families Are Dying of Crack', *New York Times*, 11 Aug. 1989 (p. A1).
21. ibid.
22. R. C. Harruff, J. T. Francisco *et al.*, 'Cocaine and Homicide in Memphis and Shelby County: An Epidemic of Violence, *Journal of Forensic Science* 33(5): 1231–7 (1988).
23. Associated Press, *New Haven Register*, 15 Aug. 1989 (p. 1).
24. J. Johnson, 'Drug Gangs Are Now Operating in Rural States, Justice Department Says', *New York Times*, 4 Aug. 1989.
25. M. McConnell, 'Crack Invades the Countryside', *Readers Digest*, February 1989 (pp. 73–8).
26. M. Miller, 'A Jamaican Invasion in West Virginia', *Newsweek*, 28 March 1988, p. 24.
27. S. H. Verhovek, 'Drug-Related Arrests Climbing in Suburban and Upstate New York', *New York Times*, 14 Aug. 1989.
28. J. F. Jekel and D. F. Allen, 'Trends in Drug Abuse in the Mid-1980s', *Yale Journal of Biology and Medicine* 60: 45–52 (1987).
29. ibid.
30. J. C. McKinley, Jr., 'Police Seize Vial Machines Tied to Crack', *New York Times*, 25 April 1990.
31. T. Morganthau, 'Crack and Crime', *Newsweek*, 107(24): 22 (1986).
32. 'Space Basing: A Perilous New Connection', *Newsweek*, 107(26): 53 (1986).
33. The White House, *National Drug Control Strategy*, Sept. 1989, p. 3.
34. ibid, p. 1.
35. M. D. Bianchi and A. L. Hampson (eds), *Poems by Emily Dickinson* (Boston: Little, Brown, 1950), p. 19.

2 Crack Addiction: A Clinical Perspective

The complexity of crack addiction is compounded by the different methods of use, the widespread vulnerability of the general population, and the subtlety of the outward symptoms in the early stages, making detection difficult. This chapter provides an overview of the modes of action of crack cocaine and of the clinical effects of addiction to it.[1]

MODES OF ACTION OF CRACK COCAINE

Feelings of pleasure and well-being (euphoria) normally occur when certain external stimuli cause the release of dopamine, a chemical transmitter, in the pleasure centers in the brain. Dopamine is released when the sending nerve is stimulated. The chemical crosses the microscopic space between nerve cells, and when the receiving nerve ending is touched by the neurotransmitter, it is stimulated to fire. Then, ordinarily the dopamine in the space between the nerves is reabsorbed by the sending nerve, by a kind of microscopic 're-uptake pump'. Thus the stimulation of the next nerve is brief, and the supply of dopamine is conserved. Cocaine blocks the re-uptake of dopamine which therefore remains in the synapse, continuing to stimulate the next nerve, which soon becomes over-stimulated.

The constant stimulation eventually depletes the sender cells of dopamine, because dopamine synthesis cannot keep pace with the dopamine release. Because the production of dopamine is eventually exhausted, the nerves become understimulated, and the negative late effects of crack (feeling bad, depressed, with little energy or ability to experience pleasure – all part of the 'dysphoria') begin to appear. These and other mechanisms provide the physiologic reasons for the initial euphoria and the subsequent dysphoria which crack abusers experience.

DYNAMICS OF CRACK ABUSE

In snorting cocaine hydrochloride, about 25–30 per cent of the cocaine enters the brain over a 5–15 minute period, causing a gradual development of euphoria (the 'high'), which tapers off in 10–20 more minutes. Obviously the strength and duration of this high will be affected by the amount and purity of the cocaine used, and the frequency of its use.

In smoking crack, about 80 per cent pure cocaine passes into the brain, with a very sudden and powerful 'high' being felt as a 'hit' 8–12 seconds after starting to inhale the crack. This can be one of the most pleasurable experiences known. However, the massive release of dopamine depletes the nerve cells, making it difficult to achieve the same level of euphoria with repeated smoking of crack.

The initial high acts as a *positive* reinforcement, because the memory of it causes users to try repeatedly to duplicate the initial high. Partly because of dopamine depletion, the subsequent highs usually are less intense and of shorter duration. Moreover, eventually the addict no longer returns to 'normal' after smoking crack, but begins to 'crash' (go from the euphoria not to normal but to bad feelings – dysphoria). The result is an increasingly severe crack depression which acts as a *negative* reinforcement, causing the user to seek more crack.

Both the continual search for the original high, and the attempt to avoid depression, lead to binging on crack. Binging involves repeated administration of crack, producing frequent mood changes. Binges may continue for up to seven days, with the user getting minimal food, and the binge usually will continue until all available crack is used.[2] During this time the addict is unpredictable; some will do anything – including stealing, prostitution, or killing – to obtain more crack. Unlike with alcohol or opiates, the absence of daily use of crack may not indicate a less severe problem. In fact, the most severe form of crack addiction tends to be characterized by days of binging followed by days of abstinence, and then more binges and periods of abstinence.

The good feelings are a positive reinforcement to more crack use, and the crash (including depression and craving) which occurs on cessation of use, is a negative reinforcement for compulsive cocaine use. Although it lacks the severe physical withdrawal effects of opiates or sedatives, crack use results in severe craving. Crack addiction, then, according to Dakis and Gold, is an interplay of positive and negative reinforcements.[3] Thus crack addiction may be defined in terms of 'physiological reinforcement' rather than obvious withdrawal symptoms.

Fearing the severity of the crash, many addicts use heroin, marijuana, or hard alcohol to soften its impact. As the addict continues to use crack, the quality of the euphoric experience lessens, and the intensity of the crash deepens, throwing the addict into depression. In interviews with scores of crack addicts, many of whom have been using it for 3 years or more, most claim the high diminishes and they never again reach the original high, although it remains pleasurable for a long time. Moreover, they find they have to keep using crack to avoid 'terrible down feelings'.

Wikler has developed a model for the psychological understanding of addictive illnesses based on a behavioral approach involving classical and operant conditioning.[4] This model is helpful in understanding crack abuse. Initially the addict uses crack for any number of reasons, including curiosity, peer pressure, boredom, partying, or recreation. However, the psychological reward effects of the overwhelming high leads to repeated use of the drug to obtain further pleasure. This is clearly demonstrated by the tendency of experimental animals to self-administer intravenous cocaine to the point of death or serious toxicity.[5] The physiological mechanisms of crack abuse override the basic instincts for survival, such as hunger, thirst and sex. In response, addicts turn to compulsive use of crack to obtain pleasure and relief from craving. According to Gawin *et al.*, pulses of euphoria in a binge produce long-term memories which stimulate craving.[6] The period of non-use will continue until the memories of euphoria bombard the user, causing cravings which lead to use.

Depending on the availability and accessibility of crack, many early addicts move quickly to compulsive use. The most difficult part of crack addiction to treat is the cravings, intense urges for the drug manifested by a variety of phenomena: physical (anxiety, sweating, palpitations, stomach pains), emotional (quickly changing moods, angry outbursts), mental (dreaming or constant thinking about crack), social (intense feelings of loneliness and isolation), and spiritual (feeling of emptiness or boredom or the lack of meaning in life) phenomena.

The cravings may be brought on by stimuli that are linked with positive crack use in the past.[7] These include experiences concerning moods, people, locations, and other intoxicants or objects such as money, white powders, pipes, and syringes.[8] Effective treatment of crack addiction depends on the successful management of craving symptoms. Extinction of the potency of cravings occurs when the conditioned cues are continuously frustrated and not rewarded with crack. A number of medications have recently been shown to be effective in treating craving: e.g., desipramine, bromocriptine, and injection of flupenthixol decanoate.

PHYSICAL SYMPTOMS

Crack abuse can lead to symptoms and major complications in many of the body systems. Some of the most common are listed below.

The respiratory system
Inhalation of pure cocaine vapor into the lungs leads to an increased incidence of bronchitis with black bloody exudates, chest pain, pneumonia, and reactivation of tuberculosis. Whether or not crack smoking can produce long-term respiratory illness or cause lung cancer is unclear.

The gastrointestinal system
Crack depresses the appetite center in the brain, causing anorexia and loss of weight. Often this is associated with deficiencies in such vitamins as thiamine, pyridoxine, and ascorbic acid, and an increased incidence of infections.

The cardiovascular system
Crack has a stimulating effect on the heart which may cause abnormal rhythms (including the usually fatal ventricular fibrillation), coronary heart disease, and severe palpitations. One addict described a sensation of his heart 'jumping out of his skin' while using crack.

The central nervous system
Upon crossing the blood-brain barrier, crack stimulates and may irritate the brain substance causing severe convulsions. In a typical case, the disintegration of a plastic sheath, used to transport cocaine in the stomach of a courier, will release a lethal dose of cocaine into the body, causing agitation, severe convulsions, and

death. Cocaine use in any form causes hypertension and can lead to cerebral hemorrhages.

The skin
Crack addicts sometimes experience severe itching over the body, especially in the limbs. Repeated scratching may cause lines of sores along the limbs. Coloquially this severe itching is called the 'cocaine bug'.

Pregnancy
Work by Chasnoff *et al.* has shown that cocaine-using women have a higher rate of spontaneous abortion than women in other groups. Also there seems to be an increased rate of abruptio placenta. Some infants exposed to cocaine have significant depression of interactive behavior and poor response to environmental stimuli.[9]

The endocrine system
Initially the crack high causes hypersexuality, which may be followed by impotence. In some cases, the hypersexuality is manifested in a polymorphous sexuality where 'anything and anybody becomes a turn-on'. Some female crack addicts describe a galloping sexuality which leads them to associate crack and sex, and they may end up in prostitution in order to support their habit. Eventually crack leads to severe sexual dysfunction, including impotence and the inability to experience sexual pleasure without cocaine.

Death
Cohen[10] has outlined a number of ways a cocaine addict may die. These include:

Overdose. In binge-crack smoking, an addict may increase the size of the crack dose, with higher concentrations of cocaine entering the blood and brain. This may lead to depression of the respiratory center or ventricular fibrillation of the heart.

Hypersensitivity to cocaine. Cocaine is rapidly broken down by enzymes in the liver and blood; even small amounts of cocaine may cause death in persons with congenital absence of these enzymes.

Major convulsions. Convulsions caused by crack use may lead to death through status epilepticus.

Coronary heart disease. The blood vessel constrictor effect of cocaine may decrease coronary blood supply and cause heart attacks.

Depression of the respiratory center. The respiratory center is depressed by the combination of cocaine and heroin (speedball). Although cocaine is a stimulant, in large doses it depresses the respiratory center, as does heroin.

Homicide. The paranoid ideation and behavior of crack addicts may lead to murder. Our experience indicates that crack releases aggressions, with violent consequences.

Accidental death. Crack use gives drivers a false sense of competence, causing them to take foolish risks which may lead to traffic fatalities. One study found that ' . . . nearly one out of four New York City drivers aged 16 to 45 who died in motor vehicle accidents during three years in the mid-1980s had used cocaine within 48 hours of death'.[11]

Immune deficiencies. In some addicts persistent malnutrition and emaciation can lead to a worsening of viral and bacterial infections, such as hepatitis B and tuberculosis.

Suicide. After binges, addicts may become so severely depressed that they kill themselves.

PSYCHOLOGICAL EFFECTS

Crack cocaine neurochemically magnifies the pleasure of most activities. Early in its use it may increase confidence, alertness, and self-esteem, and create a sense of well being associated with increased energy levels and decreased social inhibitions. In some ways crack produces the feelings of being the desired image of western life – i.e., slim, cool, confident, and successful. As one young crack addict stated, 'When I have a hit, I feel like I own the world. As I walk down the street, it all belongs to me'.

In snorting cocaine, this sense of well-being could predominate for months or years before depression occurred, but with crack, the user often begins to show signs of psychopathology within three to six months. A number of patients have shared with us that they snorted for years without ill-effects, but developed anxiety and paranoid thinking after three or four months of crack use.

The first signs of emotional decompensation are depressed feelings and loss of the ability to get pleasure. Losing interest in the basic pleasures of life, the addict seeks refuge in more crack use. Eventually the bad feelings lead to a cocaine withdrawal depression, manifested by insomnia, weakness, sadness, social isolation, and loss of interest in work. In this state, the addict is on edge and spends all his time contemplating how to get more crack. Addicts claim that as craving intensifies, such objects as gold, jewelry, money, and electronic equipment, which are easily pawned, become synonymous with crack. Stealing these objects from strangers, families, or friends happens automatically, without compunction.

As the addiction increases in severity, a type of instinctual fragmentation occurs during which many addicts forego such normal pleasures as sex, eating, and drinking because of the preoccupation with crack. This sometimes leads to serious weight loss, causing the physical condition to deteriorate to a dangerous level. Further psychological decompensation leads to paranoid ideas and behavior. This may vary from mild, e.g. the feeling of being watched by a policeman, to more severe, when the addict, fearing that he might be killed by a drug-using colleague, murders him instead.

Cocaine psychosis was thought to be unusual until recently.[12] Manschrek *et al.*, in a study of 106 cases of hospitalized crack patients in 1985, found that 29 per cent had evidence of psychosis, and 16 per cent had a history of transient psychosis (i.e. of less than 24 hour duration).[13] They described two types of psychoses: (a) *an acute onset psychosis* with confusion, and associated with the use of high doses of crack over a short period of time, and (b) *an insidious onset psychosis* manifested by diverse psychopathology, brought on by heavy crack use over long periods of time.

In the Bahamas, chronic crack abusers describe various types of crack psychoses as 'high base craziness' and 'low base craziness'. (Because crack is the freebase form of cocaine, it is sometimes called just 'base' on the streets). Having had the opportunity to study their behavior in 'base camps' (the Bahamian equivalent of American 'base houses'), our understanding of these phenomena is as follows: 'High base craziness' (acute onset psychosis) involves a sudden experience of widespread auditory hallucinations, when everything in the environment of the addict speaks to him. For example, a young man described how, after smoking crack, he went to his closet to get his clothes, but his suit asked him, 'What do you want?' Afraid, he walked toward the door, which told him, 'get back!' Retreating, he then heard the sofa say, 'If you sit on me, I'll kick your . . .'. With a sense of impending doom, intense anxiety, and mounting panic, the young man ran to the hospital, where he received help. This is a very frightening experience, and recovered addicts continue to dread the experience even after treatment.

In 'low base craziness' (insidious onset psychosis) the addict searches the ground on his hands and knees seeking crack cocaine in a ritualistic fashion. In a state of delusion, the addict picks up any object even remotely appearing to be crack (e.g. pieces of stone, wood, garbage, and other unsanitary materials) and tries to smoke them in his pipe or camoke. While visiting a base camp in the woods, one of the authors observed crack addicts living in make-shift homes made out of wooden boxes. Outside of one of these structures was an unkempt, malnourished woman attempting to smoke crack. After a while she was on her knees clearing away brush, picking at debris on the ground, and mumbling that the police were out to get her.

Low-low depression

Besides the common crack withdrawal depression, a more severe depression is found in crack addicts who have used increasing quantities of cocaine over a period of 10 to 24 months. In this condition, which we describe as the low-low depression, the user is depressed with persistent thoughts of suicide. According to them, the depression is like a thick dark cloud which descends on them and death appears to be the only way out. The phenomenon tends to occur shortly after a crack binge. Even close friends find it difficult to assess the severity and urgency of this situation and may not realize the addict is in danger of suicide.

A Case Example.
A young man who made a number of attempts at treatment, persisted in returning to crack use. Previously he was well-dressed and groomed, but he became less interested in his personal appearance and moved from prestigious jobs to low status jobs. One night during dinner with his family, he asked to be excused. An hour later he was found hanging dead in the closet of his room. He left a note to his family: 'I love you very much, but I can't beat cocaine'.

It is not known whether this severe depression is a separate entity. Perhaps it is due to the extreme damage to the neuro-reward centers of the brain, causing psychological collapse. It is known that in this state a person can become suicidal, homicidal, or manifest some other bizarre behavior to cope with, or defend against, his sense of impending doom. Much research is needed in this area.

SOCIAL EFFECTS

Besides the physical and psychological consequences of crack addiction, the social impact on the addict's life may be devastating. Crack cocaine is a no-barrier drug which creates havoc in persons from all segments of the socio-economic spectrum. Once the user is addicted, the mind is constantly thinking of crack. Hence every sleeping dream, every waking thought, every motivation and ambition is how to obtain more crack. Compulsive crack use is associated with ethical fragmentation, in which the user loses his conscience and other moral influences. At this point, anything may be tried: prostitution, promiscuity, sado-masochistic behaviors, stealing, lying, bestiality, etc. This phenomenon may occur even in people who previously were well organized, with excellent family backgrounds, good education, and professional training. The ability for good judgment may be destroyed. For example, a young executive secretary rushed into a cocaine treatment clinic begging for help because she had just sold her $10,000 car for $80 and the euphoria had only lasted for a short time.

Crack cocaine has a powerful disintegrating effect on family life, causing much pain and anguish for family members. It destroys even the maternal instinct. The authors have encountered mothers who left their children unattended for days in the home. We have seen fathers use their total week's wages on crack, causing the children to go hungry. But perhaps most painful is to see parents, especially the mothers, blame themselves for the children's addiction, and, in severe cases, even commit suicide.

Chronic crack addiction and violent crime

As the crack cocaine epidemic spreads, perhaps the most worrisome spectacle is the plight of the chronic addict. As is to be expected, the longer a crack problem exists in a community, the more chronic addicts there will be. These tend to be young men and women who have used crack for 3–5 years; they may or may not have made one or more attempts at treatment. Dropouts from society, they may appear haggard, live in unsanitary conditions, suffer from vitamin deficiencies, and have a higher incidence of many chronic diseases. As a result of central nervous system impairment, they are agitated, have poor concentration, low frustration tolerance, and suffer from concrete and paranoid thinking; they are unable to hold down a proper job.

Suffering from severe dopamine depletion in the pleasure pathways of the brain, chronic crack addicts receive 'highs' of diminishing intensity but face increasing bouts of cocaine depression. They will do almost anything to obtain crack, including begging, doing odd street jobs, stealing, and prostitution or violent crime. As a result, chronic addicts, unable to obtain the 'high' they once experienced, continue to use crack to produce only a transient, mild sense of well being, which is their only escape.

As has been shown in the United States and the Bahamas, there is an association between chronic crack addiction and violent crime. In the United States in 1986, a survey of state prisoners found that one in ten was under the influence of cocaine at the time of the crime. This is more than twice the number in 1979, before the onslaught of crack cocaine. Similarly, more than half the males arrested in nine major cities in the United States tested positive for cocaine last year. In Washington DC the figure was 59 per cent, up 14 per cent from 1984. In Manhattan, the figure was more than 80 per cent.[14]

In 1987 a United States survey found that police classified more than a third of murders and two-thirds of robberies and burglaries as drug-related.[15] Anyone working closely with crack addicts will quickly learn about the close association between crack and violent crime. Increasingly, the chronic crack addict has a tendency to end up in prison rather than a treatment program, because of violent crime. Refusing to come voluntarily for help, or unable to afford or find it, they are often forcibly incarcerated because of their crimes. A recent survey at the cocaine treatment center in the Bahamas indicated that more than one-third of the patients had been involved in some type of violent crime.[16]

Conditioned cues

Besides the normal biological craving of cocaine withdrawal, the chronic crack addict experiences a superimposed, episodic craving or sensation based on exposure to conditioned cues (which may be objects, feelings, places, or persons) associated with the memory of the euphoric experience. Reminding the addict of the high they got from crack, these cues produce a powerful sensation of stimulation, similar to a cocaine high, but without euphoria. Overwhelmed by a sensation of craving for the missing euphoria, the addict may be drawn to steal. Upon pawning what was stolen, the addict discovers that the 'high' received from the cocaine is not as powerful as the anticipated high stimulated by seeing the cue (watch, etc.).

Psychopathology due to crack cocaine

In the Manschreck *et al.* study mentioned above, which showed considerable psychosis in the crack abusers, they found that 55 per cent of the addicts with crack-induced psychosis had been involved in some type of violent behavior.[17]

Of the crack addicts who were non-psychotic but suffered from depression and anxiety, 35 per cent had been involved in violent behavior. This study validates the clinical impression that psychopathology due to crack cocaine is associated with violent behavior. In fact, with the possible exceptions of amphetamines and phencyclidine (PCP), crack has a greater violence-stimulating potential than other abused drugs. One can understand the chaos in Washington DC, where crack cocaine often is used with PCP ('space basing'), which produces an extreme potential for violence.

Sociocultural fragmentation

An increase in chronic crack addiction in an area is associated with a concomitant breakdown in values of respect for persons and property. In such situations, crack is the desired end, and obtaining it and controlling the drug supply becomes the foremost ambition. This leads to the proliferation of youth gangs, open peddling of drugs, and violent crime. The inner cities of New York, Washington, and Los Angeles are prime examples of this phenomenon.

In conclusion, it is obvious that crack addiction is a multifaceted problem, defying simplistic solutions and unresponsive to empty platitudes. Promising good feelings, it results in an increasing dysphoria, which dehumanizes and destroys the person.

References

1. D. F. Allen, *Modes of use, precursors and indicators of cocaine abuse in the cocaine crisis*, edited by D. F. Allen (New York: Plenum Press 1987), pp. 15–25.

2. F. H. Gawin and E. H. Ellinwood, 'Cocaine and other stimulants, actions abuse and treatment', *New England Journal of Medicine*, vol. 316, no. 18, p. 1175.
3. C. A. Dakis and M. Gold, 'New Concepts in Cocaine Addiction: The Dopamine Depletion Hypothesis', *The Clinical Psychiatric Quarterly Newsletter*, The American Academy of Clinical Psychiatrists, 9(3), (1986).
4. A. Wikler and R. Pescor, 'Classic Condition of a Morphine Abstinence Phonomenon Reinforcement of Opioid Drinking Behavior and Relapse in Morphine Addicted Rates', *Psychopharmacologia* 10: 255–84 (1967).
5. C. E. Johanson, 'Assessment of the Dependence Potential of Cocaine in Animals', National Institute on Drug Abuse, Research Monograph Series 50 (Washington DC: US Government Printing Office, 1984) pp. 54–71.
6. Gawin and Ellinwood, op. cit.
7. F. H. Gawin, D. F. Allen, and B. Humblestone, 'Outpatient treatment of 'crack' cocaine smoking with flupenthixol decanoate', *Arch. Gen. Psychiatry* vol. 46, April 1989.
8. Gawin and Ellinwood, op. cit.
9. I. J. Chasnoff, D. R. Griffith, S. MacGregor, *et al.*, 'Temporal patterns of cocaine use in pregnancy. Perinatal outcome', *Journal of the American Medical Association* 261(12): 1741–4 (24 March 1989).
10. S. Cohen, *Cocaine: The Bottom Line*, The American Council for Drug Education, 1985.
11. 'Cocaine danger on the road', *Science News* 137:23, 13 January 1990.
12. T. C. Manschrek, D. F. Allen, and M. Nevelle, 'Freebase psychosis: cases from a Bahamian epidemic of cocaine abuse', *Comprehensive Psychiatry* vol. 28, no. 6 (Nov.–Dec. 1987), pp. 555–64.
13. T. C. Manschrek, J.A. Langhery, C. C. Weisstein, D. F. Allen, B. Humblestone, M. Neville, H. Podlewski, N. Mitra, 'Characteristics of freebase cocaine psychosis', *Yale Journal of Biology and Medicine* 61 (1988), pp. 115–22.
14. 'Crack', *New York Times*, 'Week In Review' Section, 28 May 1989, p. 14.
15. ibid.
16. This survey was done at the cocaine treatment program at Knowles House and the Haven, in Nassau in the Bahamas.
17. Manschrek *et al.*, 'Characteristics of . . . ', op. cit.

3 Crack Addiction in the Home, School, and Workplace

Early in the development of crack addiction, the signs may not be obvious for even the most observant parent, teacher, or employer. It is only through being alert to the early clues that one is able to detect the problem. This chapter discusses the early signs of crack abuse and other phenomena that may assist the detection of the problem in the home, the school, and the workplace.

It is a sad experience to meet parents whose children have been using drugs for a long time, often for more than two years, without their knowledge. An erudite, successful businessman contacted one of the authors claiming that his son had become rebellious, distant, and unmanageable. He said that money around the home would disappear and, more recently, valuable objects from his office were missing. When the son was interviewed in the presence of the father, the son admitted to using crack for the previous two years. The parent, shocked, exclaimed, 'I wish I had known! How could I have picked it up?'

Stories like this abound, with parents expressing guilt and anger. A lady in Ohio whose son was a severe crack addict said, 'How come no one told me about this? Shouldn't the government have educated us about this tragedy?' The ignorance about the problem of drug abuse is compounded by strong denial mechanisms, which prevent parents from recognizing the problem and responding appropriately. In our experience, crack is a drug of all classes of society, and once it appears in a particular neighborhood, anyone is vulnerable. It is a drug which must not be tried even once, because we have interviewed scores of persons who claim they started on the road to addiction after their first high.

SIGNS OF CRACK ABUSE

The detection of crack abuse is difficult because the addiction usually is far advanced by the time known signs are evident. In our experience, a person may have snorted cocaine for up to two years or more before deterioration occurs. Clinical deterioration occurs much more rapidly in the case of crack, usually in a three to six month period. Signs which may indicate cocaine abuse in a family member include the following:

Staying out all night or missing school or work

These habits, if atypical of an individual, are suggesting of cocaine or other drug use.

Changes in personality

Any sudden change in personality may indicate cocaine abuse. For example, a quiet reserved person may become loud and outgoing, or vice versa. Other personality changes include the development of argumentativeness, combativeness, and irrationality.

Other changes in behavior

Not all cocaine-related changes are initially seen as bad, and 'positive' changes do not rule out crack use. In the initial stages, the person on crack may become more confident, productive, and show improved performance at home, school, or at work. For example, a mother said that initially her son, who used to be lazy, changed to being extremely helpful around the house, such as by washing dishes, scrubbing floors, and mowing the lawn. It was not until her television set suddenly disappeared that she suspected drug abuse. Other indicative behaviors include extreme aggressiveness and even violence, paranoid behavior, or total isolation, especially if these are unusual for the individual.

Ethical fragmentation

Crack addicts appear to become detached from previous values and controls of conscience. As a result, they have less conflict about stealing, lying, promiscuity, or prostitution. Such concepts as loyalty to family or friends – or responsibility to others – decrease in importance in comparison to obtaining more crack; that is, all previous values and value systems become subordinated to crack.

Change in associations

Early addiction to crack is communal, and this sooner or later becomes evident. The parent or spouse may notice an entirely new group of friends. Similarly, telephone calls may become suspicious or threatening. In certain instances, members of the user's family may be approached or accosted by pushers for monies owed to them for the child's purchase of cocaine.

Change in work habits

Crack addicts eventually become less productive, with little interest in the quality of work or homework. In adolescents, the school grades may decline, and a once-industrious child may lose interest in school. It is important to stress that drug problems on the job or in school generally appear as low productivity, poor attitudes, chronic absenteeism, or tardiness and stealing, rather than as overt drug use behavior.

Physical signs

There are a number of key physical signs which point to a possible crack addiction. Extreme loss of body weight is one; a normally well-built person becomes very thin. As is said in the Bahamas, 'They were once a brickhouse; now they're a stickhouse!'

Intense itching in the limbs
This is called the 'cocaine bug', and is another sign. Persons with this problem are constantly scratching their arms and legs.

Irritation and sores of the mucosa of the nose
These are sometimes seen in persons who snort cocaine. In extreme circumstances, there may be actual destruction of the septum between the two sides of the nose.

Convulsions
This may be the first overt sign of crack addiction. Cocaine is

a stimulant, which may be the mechanism of the convulsions, although others have been proposed.

Persistent hacking cough with dark sputum
Crack addicts have an increased incidence of cough, colds, pneumonia, and even tuberculosis. Characteristically, they have a pungent, dark-coloured, blood-tinged sputum.

Scaly skin
The lack of nutrition and tendency to scratch may be associated with scaly skin and sores.

Tired or blurry eyes
Crack addicts may participate in binges around the clock and, as a result, appear spaced out, with tired or blurry eyes. After several successive days of binging, addicts may 'crash' and sleep for days as well.

Drug paraphernalia around the home

As crack addicts become entrenched in their addiction, they become cavalier about leaving drug paraphernalia around. A parent or boss may find water pipes, crack containers (vials with different coloured caps), pieces of crack cocaine, baking soda (used to precipitate the crack cocaine from the cocaine hydrochloride), and glasses with aluminium foil (i.e., homemade smoking apparatus for smoking crack cocaine). Parents should keep informed about the different types of paraphernalia, because they are constantly being changed to avoid scrutiny by law enforcement officials and others. For example, in the Bahamas, freebase addicts have been adapting soda cans or pieces of PVC piping to make equipment for smoking crack cocaine. Certainly, water glasses with cigarette ash or foil paper are common tell-tale signs. One parent thought his son was doing chemistry experiments, only to discover that he had been smoking freebase cocaine.

Summary

No one of these signs is conclusive, except the possession of crack cocaine or drug paraphernalia. What is most important is not so much the behavior itself as a noticeable *change* in behaviour, so that the person's behaviour surprises parents, family members, or employers by being different, and the person is seen as now being different from what he or she used to be.

It is important to remember that not all behavior change, particularly in adolescents, is due to drugs. Adolescence is a stormy time for many children, and occasional outbursts do not necessarily imply drug use. More harm than good may be caused by unfounded accusations, which actually may become self-fulfilling prophecies. Teenagers may say to themselves, in effect, 'If I am going to be accused of drug abuse anyway, I might as well be doing it'. If parents or employers are suspicious, rather than deny the situation or get into an angry confrontation, it is best to have the person be seen by an expert in drug problems. A good professional will perform a thorough clinical assessment, including a urinalysis, and will then form an opinion based on the complete assessment. It must be stressed that a urine test is a medical investigation and should be used as a part of a complete clinical assessment.

Once the diagnosis is made, the professional will discuss the various options for treatment. Parents or others should explore all the options and choose the one most suited to their particular situation. The treatment of crack cocaine addiction is arduous and often frustrating for the patient and family. Therefore, once a program of treatment has been chosen, the family should be involved in the therapeutic process for education, support, and insight. This, in turn, will encourage the patient and increase the probability of a successful outcome of treatment.

THE FAMILY AND DRUGS

A common denominator of the crack epidemic is the devastation of family life and relationships that it leaves in its wake. But this is not a simple association, because even though crack addiction causes family disintegration, the intensity and widespread nature of the epidemic also may be a symptom of the pre-existing fragmentation of family life so common in modern times. Bry *et al.* have studied precursors or factors that predispose to drug abuse, such as poor family relationships, low self-esteem, absence of academic achievement.[1] These will be discussed in more detail. Due to the complex nature of drug addiction, it is likely that a multiplicity of factors, rather than a single one, cause drug abuse in a given individual. Moreover, because these factors are associated with drug abuse does not necessarily imply that they cause the problem in a given situation, although undoubtedly they do in many drug abusers. The following factors, however, have been found to be predictive in many studies; in most cases, plausible reasons for their contributing to drug abuse are evident. In the following list we have drawn upon the outline of Bry *et al.* and on our own experience in order to present precursors which may influence, directly or indirectly, the development of drug abuse in families.

Poor parent-child relationships

Conflict in the family contributes to insecurity in the child and to communication problems between parent and child, increasing the child's vulnerability to drug abuse.[2] Financial pressures, the fast pace of life, and the many pressures to conform to a powerful materialism place the average family under severe stress, weakening the security felt in the child's environment.

A secure home is an intimate environment when the parents provide stability, consistency, and predictability. The child feels safe, and psychologically internalizes the caring, supportive image of the parents, especially the mother. This internalization of the primary caring figures enables the child to move through the maturation process in the development of his or her own identity.

When parents are themselves undergoing various pressures, they may fail to provide the stability, consistency, and predictability vital to the infant's bonding process. As a result, the child may grow up with an emptiness, which manifests itself from ages ten to fifteen as low self-esteem, poor frustration tolerance, boredom, depression, and eventually often drug addiction. The drug then may become a substitute for the missing parental support which is needed for the child to form a sense of self.

In former days, most nations of the world also consisted of bonded, or mutually supportive villages and communities. There were surrogate parental figures, often other relatives, who helped to make up for any lack of structure in families, because these adults knew the children personally and provided encouragement, stimulation, and correction. Today this situation is uncommon in industrial and post-industrial societies. The family and extended family are under siege, and our neighborhoods have become isolated, polarized, even dangerous – anything but intimate and supportive.[3] In some cases, the only models for healthy family relationships are television situation comedies, such as the Cosby show.

Low self-esteem

Persons with poor self-esteem have decreased ability to cope and lower thresholds for ambiguity, frustration, and dissonance.[4] Experiencing higher levels of anxiety, hopelessness, and passivity, they find it difficult to resist drugs.

Contributing to this situation are the needs of the 'grandiose self', which is the difference between the expected self (i.e., what the parents expect of the child) and his actual self (especially, his actual abilities and accomplishments). Thus the child from ages 9 to 15 who has not lived up to his parents' expectations carries the burden of the grandiose self, which causes low self-esteem and makes him vulnerable to drug abuse.

An example of this was a young man, aged 19 years, who reported that his father had great plans for his education. However, he failed in school and was not able to obtain a high-status job. Because his father was extremely angry with him, the son lived with a deep sense of failure. Introduced to crack cocaine, he became addicted. He said the highs made him feel cool, confident, and successful, everything he really was not.

Low academic achievement

Our experience agrees with other studies that suggest there is a strong association between low academic achievement or motivation and drug abuse.[5] Low academic motivation may come from fragmented families where education is not a high priority, and studies are not encouraged.

Another modern obstacle to academic motivation and development appears to be excessive use of television, which can replace family socialization activities, such as family conversation and family games. Children who watch excessive amounts of television suffer from poor concentration, lack of initiative, and lowered frustration tolerance, and all of these contribute to poor academic motivation.

Psychological disturbances

Children suffering from illnesses such as depression or attention deficit disorder may seek to relieve their emotional pain and frustration through drugs.[6,7] These two problems may express themselves in a similar way, such as by hyperactivity, angry outbursts, and poor concentration.

A high experience-seeking tendency

In the post-industrial West, adolescents tend to be programmed to seek intense positive experiences, such as exciting events. When these experiences are not easily available, adolescents may interpret this deprivation as an actual 'low' or depressed mood. Such thinking has been prominent since the 1960s, when feeling high was a positive value equated with 'good', and feeling low was a negative value seen as something 'bad', to be avoided. This perspective encourages drug abuse when the drug produces feelings of euphoria, including special power and ability, success, etc. The 'crash' or 'low' that follows emphasizes the need to obtain more drug.

In London an 18 year old woman said to one of us that between her 12th and 18th birthdays, her only feelings of being high were when she was on drugs, and her lows were when she crashed off drugs. The most difficult thing in her recovery, she insisted, was to get used to, and accept, feelings that were neither high nor low, but in between.

Zuckerman *et al.* showed that those adolescents who scored high on scales that tested for sensation seeking were also more likely to be users of nicotine, alcohol, drugs, and to be sexually active.[8]

Low religiosity

Persons with a meaningful internalized religious faith expressed in a positive attitude toward life appear to be less vulnerable to drug abuse.[9] When life is meaningless and empty, one solution may be a tendency to try to fill that emptiness with drugs. Also, a religious community may provide a sense of support and encouragement and an internalized set of expectations that may help the individual to resist drug abuse, or help with rehabilitation, should that become necessary. In prior times, extremely impoverished communities were often bound by religious commonalities and meaning.

It is noteworthy that in the US ghettos where cocaine is available, often the community with the highest profile in crack resistance is a religious community (Muslims).

High family substance abuse

Modeling behaviors have a powerful influence on children. Thus, if there is high family substance abuse, even of nicotine or alcohol, such behavior is more likely to become internalized and acted out by the child.[10]

High peer substance abuse

Adolescents are strongly influenced by peers, often more than by parents. In the literature, and in our experience, adolescents find it very difficult to resist drugs if their peers use them.[11] In talking with young persons on crack cocaine, the most common reason given for their starting crack was curiosity, after they discovered their friends were using it.

High community availability of drugs

When drugs, particularly crack cocaine, are abundantly available, the rate of abuse increases considerably. In the US and the Caribbean, the high availability of low cost, high quality crack has contributed to the severity of the epidemic and the difficulty of stopping it.

Poverty and affluence

The lifestyle of poverty provides a negative emotional state which may lead to drug use as a way of escape, and of obtaining a sense of power and well being that escapes the individual in real life. At the other financial extreme, affluence makes drug addiction easier, because of the availability of funds, and the fact that the wealth and the fame that often accompanies it may make a person a target for people trying to sell the drug. Wealth may provide a sense of control over one's life, so that the almost universal vulnerability of people to drugs such as crack is not realized.

According to work done by Bry *et al.*, the potential risk of drug abuse is directly proportional to the number of risk factors involved.[12] Therefore, families with more than three precursors may be considered at high risk for drug abuse. This is not pejorative, but rather is a warning that the family should seek help to prevent drug addiction, if it has not already occurred. We also must emphasize that even in drug-infested areas, some adolescents with multiple risk factors do not use drugs. More research is needed to understand why this is true, so see if others could use similar strengths to remain drug free.

COCAINE ADDICTION AND THE SCHOOL

A pleasant young boy of fifteen years of age became extremely angry and refused to attend school. Although he had a fairly good academic record in the past, he became rebellious, refused to do homework, and lost interest in school. Confronted by his mother about school, he had a strong emotional outburst and left home. After he was found by the police, he was seen by one of the authors. After obtaining a history, a urine test was done, which was positive for cocaine. He was given a leave of absence from school to receive treatment. After treatment he was able to return to school, and he eventually graduated from high school and entered college.

This illustrates several of the previously mentioned signs of cocaine use: a drop in grades and interest in school, and a change in emotional reactions. In this case the parent first became suspicious, but often it is a teacher who first detects signs of possible drug abuse. This is particularly when a teacher has known a student for some time and has had a close relationship with him. Although overt crack-using behavior, such as using or selling the drug, may occur on school premises, usually the cocaine use is manifested by absenteeism and poor academic achievement (particularly if these represent a recent change in pattern), stealing or lying, emotional outbursts, or callous or indifferent attitudes. In our experience, young persons on marijuana, though frequently failing in school, do attend school and may make some effort to cope. However, when someone goes onto crack, his concentration soon is impaired, he loses interest in school and ceases attendance. The family and school must work together to detect the problem and get treatment as soon as possible. A school frequently assumes the parents are aware of a student's absenteeism or change in school performance, when actually the parents are not.

In schools where drug trafficking is widespread, school children sell to other children in the schools. In some cases they give other students free samples of drugs to enable them to attain their first high. With crack cocaine this is extremely effective, because usually after the first high the victim goes looking for more. Once addicted, the student frequently must sell drugs to maintain the habit. Children who sell drugs often have complex electronic communication gadgets, such as walkie-talkies, to enable them to keep in touch with deals and to ward off school or law enforcement authorities. Child pushers often make exhorbitant amounts of money, which is used to buy expensive vehicles, jewelry, and other possessions.

A school should do all in its power to prevent the incursion of widespread drug abuse in the school. This requires good communication between parents and teachers, and also good relationships with local law enforcement agencies.

A student assistance program could be extremely helpful in developing structured, yet simple and economical methods to deal with drug problems in the school. Because of the importance of parent-teacher communication about drug problems, it may be preferable for the program to be developed by the parent-teacher organization (PTO), or at least for this type of organization to have a strong input. It probably is best for the school or PTO to contract with an outside human service agency for the assessment process for students of concern. Financial arrangements should be specified in advance, so that if specific treatment is needed, the process of referral and payment will not cause delay in treating the child.

The Bahamas has developed a model School Assistance Program (SAP), in which all teachers are trained to identify students with problems and refer them to the SAP coordinator. The goals of the program are 1) to develop a school drug policy, and 2) to identify, refer, and assist with problems. This involves early identification of the problems and then referring the students, as well as in-school supportive groups and individual counselling and follow-up services. To be effective, such a program must be supported by top officials, including the school board, principal, and community leaders. Special emphasis should be placed on making sure that all student records are confidential.

Similar programs are developing in the US, some called Student Assistance Teams.[13] These deal with alcohol and a variety of drug abuse problems. They also emphasize the positive role of teachers in supporting students, providing education regarding substance abuse, and being alert for problems in students' families and in their own colleagues.

School drug policies

Schools should develop a drug policy before a major problem arises, so that its procedures for detecting and responding to problems will be clear to all concerned. The policy should state the school's position against drugs, and outline how the school will deal with children who use drugs. This may vary from dismissal to a period of suspension to enable the child to get help. Regardless of whether the school expels or suspends a child, it should help him to get into a good treatment program. Although there is much debate about urine testing in schools, there is general consensus that if a child is showing signs of possible drug abuse, he or she should have a urine test. It is best that such a test be a part of a general assessment by a professional.

Consultation to schools

Teachers and school officials require constant updating and education about drug abuse, because the situation changes constantly. Frequent educational sessions for the teachers are needed for the faculty to remain alert and informed about what to look for. Teachers who are concerned about a particular student or problem situation should be able to request a consultation with a knowledgable professional in order to enable them to respond appropriately and to refer a student when appropriate. In our experience, this kind of collaboration between school and human service agencies is a good way to help teachers to deal with the drug problems they face in the schools.

Referral of students

There are two basic types of referrals of students. In one, the administration may refer a student because of behavioral problems such as those mentioned above or because of increasing absenteeism and poor performance. In this situation, after the complete evaluation, the consulting agency should report the findings to the school principal or headmaster. However, if individual students choose to refer themselves for help, we believe that the therapist should not report the student's problem to the school, as long as the student is continuing to get help.

Family support

If one member of a family has a substance abuse problem, either alcohol or drugs, all of the family members are involved. As stated by one news magazine, 'Living with the craziness of addiction can be as destructive to you as it is to the addict you love'.[14] The shared agony of family members is often called 'co-dependency'. Therefore, it is as important to help the other family members as to help the addicted individual. This can be done in many ways, including individual counselling, but one of the most effective ways has proved to be self-help groups, such as Al-Anon and Adult Children of Alcoholics, in the case of alcohol abuse. Outpatient group therapy and inpatient treatment are other methods being used to help co-dependents of crack abusers.

Community care systems

Unless treatment services are available, detection and referral will be of little use. Area-wide or regional systems for community awareness, prevention programs, assessment, treatment, and follow-up care offer the promise of more effective services. Sponsorships of such programs vary. For example, the Regional Youth Substance Abuse Project of Eastern Fairfield County, Connecticut, is sponsored by the United Way agency in that area and is partly funded by the Connecticut Department of Children and Youth Services and the Robert Wood Johnson Foundation. The latter also is supporting community planning grants for other communities in the US to enable them to develop and coordinate drug treatment and education efforts; an example of this is the 'Fighting Back' program in New Haven, Connecticut.[15] They are examples of what must become more common: coordinated community-wide efforts to fight substance abuse.

CRACK AND THE WORKPLACE

As the crack epidemic spreads it is having a devastating effect on many places of work, causing low productivity, theft, chronic absenteeism, costly errors such as job-related accidents, and increasing payments of claims for health care benefits. All these factors contribute to poor employee morale and major losses to businesses each year. The advent of crack cocaine has increased the pace of spread of cocaine in the workplace.

Case Example 1
An attractive woman in her 20s had worked effectively in a leading banking institution for almost seven years. She was well liked by her colleagues and highly thought of by her supervisors. After an almost perfect attendance record, she started missing days at work, giving vague excuses of family illness or family problems. Colleagues and supervisors noticed that she was always tired and that her appearance was deteriorating. Warned and counselled by the personnel office, she denied any problems and claimed her physical deterioration was due to family stress.

Eventually money was short from daily accounting, arousing further suspicions. The combination of absenteeism, low productivity, deteriorating appearance, and missing monies led to her being referred for help. During the initial visit with the counsellor, during which the family was present, the patient broke down and admitted to using crack.

This case is typical of the effect of crack in the workplace. Despite the obvious signs of drug abuse, the employee uses strong denial and avoidance. Often it is only when the family and employer work together than consensual validation occurs and the denial system is broken.

Crack use in the workplace is usually covert, and often one only notices the effects of the drug rather than any overt drug use. Occasionally, drug paraphernalia, such as water pipes or empty crack cocaine vials, may be found in the office or in a rest room, but this is usually late-stage behavior and should not be depended upon to reveal an early problem.

Of particular concern is that the increasing use of crack will adversely affect jobs involving the public safety, such as pilots, air traffic controllers, bus, lorry, and train drivers, physicians, etc.

Case Example 2
A tip-off through a local drug hotline warned authorities in one city that an airport control tower operator was on crack. Upon being contacted, the director of the control tower ordered a thorough search of the building, which turned up two home-made drug smoking devices. Recognizing the seriousness of the problem, the director organized a meeting of all the staff with a drug abuse expert.

Upon discussion, the employees all denied knowing anything about drug abuse on the job. However, one or two of them did say that periodically they saw pieces of drug equipment lying in the rest-room. The meeting showed that although there possibly was drug abuse on the job, it was difficult to prove. The day after the meeting, a senior employee at the control tower personally consulted the drug abuse expert and admitted he was on crack cocaine. He was referred for treatment.

This case illustrates the seriousness of the problem when it affects persons charged with the public's safety. It demonstrates the importance of employers moving swiftly to confront the problem, thus creating a sense of concern and a climate of awareness, which, in turn, has the effect of making the drug user feel uneasy, vulnerable, and more open to seeking help.

Persons inexperienced with drug abusers should be careful about confronting a possible user directly. Crack addicts are sometimes paranoid and easily provoked. They quickly develop violent outbursts, and may even cause fatalities. This is another reason for developing an ongoing surveillance system for early signs of drugs, so that users may be discovered at a time when they may be less difficult to confront.

Case Example 3
At a sophisticated resort, the employer noticed that one of his employees was behaving in a bizarre manner and refused to do his work. The employer accused him of being on drugs, whereupon the employee became enraged, broke a drinking glass, and cut up the manager's face. Subsequently it was discovered that he was using crack.

This example illustrates the importance of care when confronting possible drug users. Enough persons should be present to guarantee safety during the confrontation. Employers must work with families, counsellors, and sometimes the police.

The use of urine testing

When a crack problem is ubiquitous, the use of urine testing in certain circumstances may be necessary in order to create awareness and accountability. Obviously, each business should develop its own policies and procedures regarding drug testing. We recommend that, in high cocaine use areas or in high-danger jobs, employees receive screening urine tests before employment, following by random urine tests on existing employees in high risk jobs and where else thought necessary.

Employee assistance programs

Employee Assistance Programs (EAPs) have been developed within companies (or, more often, as consulting companies hired by the large firm) to help employers deal with substance abuse and mental health problems among workers. The underlying philosophy behind EAPs is that it is less costly for companies to provide treatment for substance abusing employees than to tolerate the losses due to decreased productivity, absenteeism, and threats to efficiency and safety on the job. The goal of these programs is to help employees to achieve their optimal potential, as manifested by harmonious working relationships and increased productivity. The EAP allows the company to do what it does best, management of the business, while contracting out the clinical work of urine testing, diagnosis, and treatment to experts in the field.

Components of an Employee Assistance Program
Development of a Drug Policy. According to Weiss, 'In the absense of a clear company policy that views substance abuse as a medical disorder, there is a tendency for supervisors either to look the other way when they suspect drug use or to harass suspected employees until they quit or transfer and become someone else's problem'.[16] In the authors' experience, the development of a simple, concise, and explicit drug policy has a powerful effect on making employees aware of the company's seriousness about drugs. This in turn has a preventive impact and enhances the therapeutic effectiveness of the treatment programs for employees. A company can design a policy as simple or as detailed as it wishes, but the basic components we suggest for inclusion are:

1. Drug trafficking is strictly prohibited, and investigation by law enforcement authorities will be initiated of any employee suspected of selling drugs.
2. All potential employees will be screened by urine testing.
3. Based on established guidelines, random urine samples may be requested of existing employees.
4. Employees with drug problems will not be fired, but will be given at least one opportunity with treatment, and, if that is

successfully completed, must remain in some type of organized follow-up care.

5. Employees may be required by management to undergo evaluation by the Employee Assistance Program, but are assured that this will not result in loss of wages, nor will the employee be required to pay for the evaluation.

Consultation with Supervisors. Regular training sessions for supervisors will enable them to be more adept in picking up problems on the job and ensuring earlier referral. In our experience, the quality and effectiveness of the EAP depends heavily on the awareness and training of the supervisors.

Education of Employees. Throughout the year, open educational sessions with general employees will create and awareness to the drug problem and prepare employees to face it in themselves and in their families. In addition to the area of chemical dependency, other topics can be profitably addressed, such as depression, anger, self-esteem, etc.

Referrals. Referrals are either (a) management referrals, or (b) personal (anonymous) self-referrals. Management referrals require employees to seek consultation because of behavior that concerns management. In this type of referral, the EAP must report findings to management. When employees face their own problems and refer themselves, the EAP should not give feedback to management, as long as the employee is continuing successfully in treatment and subsequent follow-up. Some employee assistance programs are comprehensive, providing care and support not only to the employees but also to their families.

Costs. Employee assistance programs vary in their costs, but the general trend is to establish a fixed fee for allowing an employee to have a prestated number of assessment sessions (often 5 sessions), and after that, in well-designed systems, the individual employee's health insurance policy comes into effect.

Summary

In summary, employee assistance programs are a valuable resource for both a company and for their substance-using employees. By providing confidential evaluation and treatment for employees, they act as a bridge between treatment programs and the company, ensuring more effective therapy and better follow-up. As a result, treatment compliance is matched with post-treatment work performance. Finally, the EAP gives the employees with problems a chance to get their lives in order, with help. However, if employees refuse to take advantage of help offered by the EAP, they must bear the responsibility for losing their jobs.

References

1. B. Bry, 'Empirical Foundations of Family-Based Approaches to Adolescent Substance Abuse', in *Preventing Adolescent Drug Abuse: Intervention Strategies*, edited by T. S. Glyn, C. G. Leukefeld, and J. P. Ludford, National Institute on Drug Abuse, Research Monograph Series, 47 (Washington DC: US Department of HHS, PHS, ADAMHA, NIDA, 1985), p. 154ff.
2. R. H. Blum, *et al.*, 'Students and Drugs' (San Francisco: Jossey-Bass, 1970).
3. Daniel P. Moynihan, 'Toward a Post-Industrial Social Policy', *The Public Interest*, 96: 16–27, Summer 1989.
4. H. B. Kaplan, 'Antecedents of Deviant Responses: Predicting from a General Theory of Deviant Behavior', *Journal of Youth and Adolescence* 6: 89–101 (1977).
5. S. Paton, R. Kessler, and D. Kandel, 'Depressive Mood and Adolescent Illicit Drug Abuse: A Longitudinal Analysis', *Journal of Genetic Psychology* 131: 267–89 (1977).
6. G. M. Smith and C. P. Fogg, 'Psychological Antecedents of Teenage Drug Abuse', in *Research in Community and Mental Health*, vol. 1, edited by R. G. Simmons (Greenwich CT: JAI Press, 1979).
7. N. D. Noya, 'Coca Paste Effects in Bolivia', presented at the International Drug Symposium, Nassau, Bahamas, Nov. 20–22, 1985.
8. M. Zuckerman, R. S. Neary, and B. A. Brustman, 'Sensation seeking Scale Correlates in Experiences (Smoking, Drugs, Alcohol, Hallucinations, and Sex) and Preference for Complexity (Design)', in *Proceedings of the 78th Annual Convention of the American Psychological Association*, vol. 5 (Washington DC: American Psychological Association, 1970).
9. F. A. Tennant, Jr, R. Detels, and V. Clarke, 'Some Childhood Antecedents of Drug and Alcohol Abuse', *American Journal of Epidemiology* 102: 377–85, 1975.
10. D. B. Kandel, 'Convergencies in Prospective Longitudinal Surveys of Drug Use in Normal Populations', in *Longitudinal Research on Drug Use: Empirical Findings and Methodological Issues*, edited by D. B. Kandel (New York: Hemisphere, 1978), pp. 3–38.
11. D. B. Kandel, D. Treiman, R. Faust, and E. Single, 'Adolescent Involvement in Legal and Illegal Drug Use: a Multiple Classification Analysis', *Social Forces* 55: 438–58, 1976.

12. B. Bry, op. cit.
13. *US News & World Report*, 11 Sept. 1989 (p. 73).
14. Ibid.
15. From materials produced by the Regional Youth Substance Abuse Project of Eastern Fairfield County (CT) and the New Haven (CT) 'Fighting Back' project.
16. R. D. Weiss, and S. M. Mirin, *Cocaine* (New York: Ballantine Books, 1987).

4 The Treatment of Crack Addiction

The treatment and rehabilitation of crack-addicted persons is difficult and frustrating, requiring tolerance and compassionate understanding. This is partly due to the widespread availability of the drug, the powerful marketing strategies used to sell it, and the strong craving experienced by the addicts.[1] Treatment is usually conducted in psychiatric facilities or in ongoing drug and alcohol treatment programs.

Treatment programs and the treatment process are discussed in this book to enable the reader better to understand the profound effect of the drug, to understand the difficulties faced by the treatment programs should someone they know require treatment, and to assist the reader, either as family member or as a professional, to work more closely with the treatment process should they need to do so.

WHO COMES FOR TREATMENT?

Much is being learned about how to treat crack addicts, but only some people with crack abuse come for treatment. Those who do so probably have more motivation to stop using the drug than those who do not. Therefore, claims of success need to be interpreted with caution when the overall problem is being considered. This chapter considers treatment for those who seek it, not for the unknown number who do not seek treatment, either because they are in jail or for other reasons.

THE GOAL OF TREATMENT

It might be said that 'patients bring their own treatment plans with them' – that is, the treatment must be designed to include the needs, goals, hopes, and fears of each patient, building on that person's strengths and insights.

There is general agreement that in order to help addicts to achieve a drug-free lifestyle, treatment must foster their development as whole persons. This requires that patients be treated with dignity and as a part of families and communities, by involving their families in treatment whenever possible. A new therapeutic community may need to be created for the patient, who must be encouraged, at the appropriate time, to return to suitable community support groups.

Vocational training and/or guidance also may be a part of the treatment program. Dr. Charles Schuster, Director of the National Institute on Drug Abuse, USA, was quoted as saying that the lesson learned in treating people addicted to other drugs such as heroin is that ' . . . the best predictor of success is whether the addict has a job'.[2] It is best if the addict already has a good job to which they can return, but providing job skills to those who lack them also is thought to help in rehabilitation.

THE PRINCIPLES OF TREATING CRACK ADDICTS

Many of the basic principles of treatment are generally agreed upon. Gawin and Ellinwood summarized the main phases of treatment in the *New England Journal of Medicine* as (a) the *initiation of abstinence* (disrupting the binge cycle) and (b) the *prevention of relapse*.[3] Methods to assist these phases include peer support groups, individual therapy with the prescribing of anti-craving drugs if needed, urine monitoring, family counselling, and educational sessions. Hospitalization is used only when necessary. Kleber emphasized that addicts must be given a place in a family and social structure which they may never have had before, that is, ' . . . habilitation more than rehabilitation'.[4] 'Habilitation' includes enabling an addict to learn the value of, and how to contribute to, groups that support each other in times of difficulty. For those who have never been a part of a close, supportive family or other group, this is a new experience.

Effective programs appear to have several distinct but carefully coordinated phases or steps: detoxification (if needed), extended personal counselling, and community support groups.[5] The second phase can vary considerably regarding the amount of time in individual counselling sessions as against how much is done through various types of therapeutic groups.

This chapter describes in detail the cocaine abuse treatment program developed in the Bahamas by one of us (DFA), partly because we are more familiar with it than with any other program, partly because of its relatively long history (the crack cocaine epidemic began in the Bahamas in 1983), and partly because it was developed in a transitional nation with limited resources, and therefore it may be more widely generalizable to non-affluent communities and to other countries than programs requiring a greater input of resources might be. The Bahamian program has achieved comparable success rates to most other programs with a relatively low input of professional resources, primarily through the heavy reliance on outpatient therapeutic groups, which depend mostly on recovering addicts in a later stage of recovery who help those addicts who are in an earlier stage.

INPATIENT OR OUTPATIENT TREATMENT?

No single method of treatment is suitable for all crack addicts. Each person is unique and has to be individually assessed regarding whether outpatient or inpatient treatment is more suitable. The authors believe that treatment and rehabilitation should be in the outpatient setting unless definite indications for inpatient treatment exist.

Underlying the conviction that outpatient treatment should be considered first is the absence of severe, medically dangerous physical withdrawal symptoms in crack abuse (although there are strong psychological withdrawal symptoms). Therefore, unlike with alcohol or heroin abuse, no substitute medicine or gradual detoxification process is needed. The depression, sleeplessness, and loss of energy and pleasure that are associated with cocaine withdrawal, if severe, can usually be treated with heterocyclic antidepressants, or, in some cases, with low doses of injected flupenthixol decanoate. Hospitalization is not usually required for the acute phase of treatment; the indications for starting with inpatient treatment are given below.

Outpatient services are less expensive, more accessible, and less stigmatized. According to Gawin, 'Outpatient treatment is often successful. Thirty to ninety per cent of abusers who remain in programs of outpatient treatment with a range of psychotherapeutic orientations stop using stimulants (cocaine) while in treatment'.[6] However, because of the lack of long-term follow-up studies, it is difficult to say categorically that outpatient treatment is better than inpatient treatment.

Outpatient services should be available to as wide a population as possible and be established in strategic locations to provide easy access for those being treated. Usually outpatient treatment is less disruptive to the life of the patient in his family, community, and job settings. Providing treatment in the open community allows patients to face the realities both of drug availability and exposure to conditioned cues that tempt them to use more crack. A study by Rawson et al. suggested that outpatient treatment is more successful because the addict has to contend and deal with the conditioned cues.[7] Although concerned that Rawson's study is flawed by self-selection of patients, Gawin agrees that reducing the craving and achieving recovery cannot occur in an environment devoid of cues.[8] Achievement of drug-free status in the community is the critical test of therapy. One recovering crack addict, who was successfully treated in the outpatient setting, remarked, 'I knew from the beginning that if I could not conquer it as an outpatient I was only fooling myself, because I have to live in the community'.[9]

Criteria for inpatient treatment

Although we favour outpatient treatment as the first approach, a good inpatient program is required as a backup for the outpatient program. Patients are referred for inpatient treatment if one or more of the following are true for them: (1) they have poor psychosocial support from their family and community; (2) there is underlying psychiatric illness or violent or suicidal tendencies; (3) there is a history of dealing in drugs as well as using them; (4) if severe withdrawal symptoms are present because of polydrug involvement (e.g., crack and alcohol or heroin); (5) if the patient has a severe crack-induced psychosis; (6) if there is a history of long term crack use in a patient with poor ego strengths; or (7) if the patient has had repeated outpatient therapy which has failed.

In these cases, inpatient treatment is continued beyond the withdrawal period and may require from three to six months. The major goal of inpatient care is to protect the patient from exposure to the drug while treatment is directed to ensure that the re-entry into society is successful and occurs with the help of family and community support. Inpatient treatment is not sufficient alone. Our experience with chronic crack users is that they ultimately require long term (i.e., more than one year) out-patient care in a program that provides values or spiritual direction, remedial education, physical exercise, and vocational training or guidance. A major goal is to help the chronic users to gain usable job skills and to develop a community socialization network. We have been impressed with the role that churches and self-help groups, such as Narcotics Anonymous and Alcoholics Anonymous, can play in the reintegration of patients into society. Half-way houses of various types also play an important role in helping addicts who have poor psychosocial support to be reintegrated into the community.

TREATMENT PROGRAM COMPONENTS

Regardless of the setting chosen for treatment, the basic components of treatment are similar, although adapted in detail to the needs and strengths of each patient. The consensus is that the most effective programs have several dimensions and offer: a variety of psychotherapeutic methods, chemotherapy if needed, self-help groups, treatment contracts with penalties for breaking the contract, urine monitoring, family therapy, education, and restriction of access to money, drug paraphernalia, and drug-using friends.

Although there is general agreement regarding the principles and settings for the treatment of crack abuse, optimal treatment design is controversial, and the actual programs that exist vary considerably. This is inevitable because of the variation in resources available, the types and numbers of therapists available to a program, and the extent of community and family support generally available. The most important points illustrated by the Bahamian program to be discussed are the value of having a planned, multiple-component program with close and continual ties to families and to the community.

The four basic components of any treatment program are:[10]

1. Assessment;
2. Abstinence initiation;
3. Relapse prevention; and
4. Long term follow-up.

The methods by which these four components are achieved can vary considerably from place to place, and the Bahamian program is only used to illustrate these components, and not to be considered

Table 4.1   Time-related structure and transitions in the cocaine treatment program of the Community Psychiatry Clinic, Nassau, Bahamas.

STAGE	STRUCTURE	DURATION	PARALLEL
I Assessment	Assessment Team	1 – 2 Days	Community Meetings
II Abstinence Initiation	a. Preparation Group b. Dynamic Abstinence Group	2 Weeks 3 – 6 Months	Community Meetings
III Relapse Prevention	Relapse Prevention Group	3 Months	Community Meetings
IV Follow-Up	Follow-up Group a. Self-help Groups b. Church Groups	2+ Years	Community Meetings

a standard by which other programs are to be judged.

The structure, sequence, and duration of each component of the Bahamian program are shown in Table 4.1. One component of the Bahamian program not commonly found in other programs is the ongoing, parallel Community Meetings, which we believe are a critical element in the overall success of the program. These community meetings give the patients an ongoing experience in reality-testing in the presence of large numbers of patients in a variety of stages of recovery.

The assessment phase

Assessment does not take long, ordinarily no more than two days, but it must be a comprehensive, multidimensional assessment. New patients are interviewed by a psychiatric team, consisting of the psychiatrist, psychologist, nurse, and social worker, in order to assess the severity of crack abuse. Particular attention is paid to the patient's physical condition to rule out medical problems such as pneumonia and head injuries. A careful mental status examination is necessary to determine if there is underlying psychiatric illness. Weiss *et al.* found that almost half of their inpatient crack users had mood disorders, from depression to bipolar (manic-depressive) illness.[11] In 1986, Gawin and Kleber validated this finding,[12] but as crack abuse has become more widespread, the proportion of new addicts with pre-existing psychiatric illness appears to have decreased. Other studies indicate that from two to five per cent of cocaine addicts in treatment have residual attention-deficit disorders.[13]

A high proportion of crack-addicted patients seeking treatment have problems with the law, with their families, or with their jobs, so that a complete psychosocial evaluation is necessary for planning treatment. Family members and significant others are encouraged to participate in the initial assessment to counteract denial by the patient and to provide verification of the problems.

The first decision to be made is whether the patient should be treated as an inpatient or an outpatient, based on the criteria listed above. Either way, the underlying physical and psychological conditions must be treated. During the first twenty-four hours after stopping crack use, the patient has intense craving for the drug, along with depression and low energy (anergia). In crack addicts, 60 to 70 per cent of those seeking treatment are emotionally fragmented and suffer from varying degrees of semi-psychotic states, often with paranoid ideas.[14] Heterocyclic antidepressants such as desipramine have been shown to counteract cocaine craving.[15] Also, bromocriptine in a single dose of 0.625mg has been shown to reduce craving, with minimal side effects.[16]

In our own experience, compliance with oral medication by crack cocaine addicts is poor, partly because antidepressants take up to two weeks or more for effective mood changes to occur. A promising new treatment involves flupenthixol decanoate. In the Bahamas, when indicated we start with a low dose of intramuscular depot flupenthixol decanoate, which acts quickly to ameliorate the craving for crack and the depression and emotional fragmentation, without exacerbating withdrawal symptoms or requiring the patient to take repeated doses of the medication. The possible value of this medication was noted in 1983, when one of us (DFA), frustrated at the time delay before the heterocyclic antidepressants suppressed the craving for crack, decided to try the more rapidly acting antidepressant flupenthixol. Over several years, dosage and frequency of administration were worked out. When used properly, flupenthixol suppressed cocaine craving quickly and had the major advantage that, because it is injected, it did not depend on the continued cooperation of the patient. Flupenthixol produces positive mood changes in one to three days and only requires administration at two to four week intervals; currently it is the subject of intensive systematic research trials.[17]

Abstinence initiation

The first goal of treatment is to break the cycle of recurrent crack use and binging. This is done by helping the addict to separate geographically and physically from the drug, and by replacing the crack-using community with an affirming, drug-free community which enhances psychosocial growth and the development of coping skills. There is much variation among different programs. We have attempted to create in the Bahamas an optimal, cost-effective program, and will use it as an example of a treatment program. In doing this we do not imply that it is the only, or even necessarily the best, program for areas with limited resources.

The basic components of the abstinence initiation phase in Nassau are: (1) Preparation Group meetings, followed by (2) Dynamic Process Group meetings, and (3) the ongoing, weekly Community Group meetings (see Table 4.1).

Preparation group meetings

The Preparation Group meetings are to engage the patients in the treatment process by improving motivation, negotiating the treatment contract, educating the patients about the addictive process, and dealing with withdrawal symptoms. A *treatment contract* is especially important. It is an agreement signed by patients promising that they will submit to urine monitoring, will be punctual and regular in team meetings, will eliminate all drug paraphernalia, will involve their family in treatment, and will dissociate themselves from drug-using friends and places. Urine testing is essential for all treatment programs, but especially in outpatient treatment. It is a tool to prevent denial, to promote self-control, and to provide an objective indicator of treatment progress.

The withdrawal symptoms mentioned above often do not require medication, but there should be no hesitation to use the medications if necessary. An effective Preparation Group provides an introduction and commitment to the treatment program and reduces the dropout rate. In some inpatient programs, the Preparation Group meetings are held prior to admission, or during the first week of admission. In outpatient programs, the preparation process may require two weeks or more before the patients are ready to be admitted to the Dynamic Process Groups, which are still a part of abstinence initiation (Table 4.1).

Dynamic process group therapy

Individual therapy is still an important adjunct to treatment, but, in the authors' experience, group therapy, where addicts are supported and confronted by peers who are not easily tricked or manipulated, is the most effective component of treatment. The frequency of these sessions varies according to the program, but we have found that holding them at least five days per week produces a powerful holding and nurturing environment for the addicts.

To help addicts initiate abstinence, they are taught to structure their daily schedules to minimize boredom and high risk situations, and they are challenged to discontinue contacts with pushers and users who are not seeking treatment. They are encouraged to share their stories in depth and receive help in the group process through modeling, education, receiving insight and support from each other, and by becoming accountable to each other.

For new addicts, the possibility of a drug-free lifestyle is reinforced by the example of patients who have been in the group for a longer period. Similarly, the more advanced patients are confronted by the pathos of the new patients, reminding them of the consequences of crack abuse. Patients are taught that the urges and cravings are natural and time-limited, and therefore they can be dealt with effectively by changing activities or talking with a drug-free friend or family member.

Beyond the biological withdrawal cravings, there are episodic craving sensations caused by receiving conditioned cues, things which the addict associates with his prior drug-using life. Conditioned cues may be such things as seeing money or jewelry, meeting or receiving a call from a former drug-using friend, seeing the old drug-using area, or any number of other things that remind the user of past highs. Of course, a sudden drug craving can occur without any known conditioned cue also. Addicts are gradually desensitized to these cues by confrontation and education, producing a kind of extinction therapy that is a major dynamic of crack abuse treatment. Addicts also are taught to use exercise and relaxation to ward off cravings.

Paradoxically, regardless of how much the crack addicts have suffered, they have a selective recall for the first high (euphoric recall) and for the good times associated with early use of the drug. This must be confronted persistently by the therapist, forcing the group to remember and reflect on the negative experiences and the destructive effects of the drug, to counteract the euphoric recall.

Community group meetings

Weekly group meetings are held throughout the program. These include the total therapeutic community, including family members, staff, and graduates of the intensive program. This provides a cohesive force to the treatment program. Using the fourteen basic steps to recovery as developed by Dr. Nelson Clarke of the Bahamas, who pioneered the development of the inpatient crack units at the Sandilands Rehabilitation Centre in Nassau, Bahamas (Appendix C), patients are challenged to recognize their powerlessness over the drug, to seek support of their peers, and to call upon spiritual resources for help.

Patients who are doing well are supported, and the community group is called upon to chastise those who do not comply with the program. Some meetings have a time of community singing, prayer, or meditation to enhance the community spirit. Often these meetings end with light refreshments and casual conversation and have the flavor of large family gatherings. Many addicts claim that the community meeting is the highlight of their treatment, because of the inspiration and feeling of being bonded together as one family. Often this is the first supportive, familial group experience for many of the patients, showing the importance of habilitation in their treatment.

Relapse prevention

After a period of abstinence maintenance to allow time for the resolution of withdrawal symptoms, patients are admitted to the Relapse Prevention Group. The goal is to make crack cocaine psychologically unavailable to the patients, since it is impossible to make it physically unavailable indefinitely. In relapse prevention, the external controls of the abstinence initiation period are reduced, while simultaneously the internal controls are strengthened. Temptations are minimized as much as possible during this process.

Often relapses are preceded by overconfident attitudes and high-risk behaviors such as visiting a crack house to rescue a friend. Similarly, addicts may begin to associate with drug-using friends, or start to smoke marijuana or drink alcohol. Emotionally, addicts may withdraw from the group and refuse to work through stressful experiences, such as rejection by a lover. Any of these situations may herald an oncoming relapse. The treatment group, along with the therapist, helps the patient gain insight into, and mastery over, these feelings.

Techniques for preventing relapse include:

1. Predicting high risk situations;
2. Learning avoidance strategies (through skits and role playing); and
3. Changing personal lifestyles to reflect meaningful values, constructive habits (such as taking responsibility for one's actions and not smoking or using alcohol), and supportive relationships in drug-free social networks.

These factors are enhanced by strengthening memories of the consequences of drug abuse, in order to counteract euphoric recall, extinguish conditional cues, and reduce external stress.[18] Alternative replacement activities, such as sports, hobbies, and community activities, further strengthen the rehabilitation process and prevent relapses. Particular emphasis is placed on self-care and reconciliation with family, community, and persons in the workplace, as the patient prepares to reenter society.

Of particular note is the 'abstinence violation effect',[19] when an addict, upon relapsing, becomes discouraged, guilty, depressed, and continues to use. Throughout the program, but particularly in the relapse prevention phase, patients are taught that relapse is always a possibility, but that a relapse is only a temporary slip if abstinence is quickly regained and one learns from experience.

Follow-up

The major issue during follow-up is for the addicts to become integrated into their local communities, where they have a sense of belonging. Resocialization of the addicts into their families and local communities is central to this. Many of the addicts learn how to function in families and communities for the first time through the treatment, and the family can do much to facilitate reentry into the community.

Halfway houses or long-term therapeutic communities are particularly helpful for hard core chronic crack addicts who have suffered total disintegration of family and community life, finding themselves in and out of prison. Such programs stress spiritual direction – the development of values and purpose in life – as well as remedial education, physical exercise, and vocational training. Once the recovering addicts develop job skills and are able to obtain jobs, their chance of long term recovery improves greatly. The combination of jobs, family support, and integration into the local community support system further improves the chances for recovery. We have observed that once addicts are firm in their recovery process, they often seek out some type of religious group or become deeply committed to self-help programs like Narcotics Anonymous.

OTHER TYPES OF DRUG PROGRAM

Many other types of drug programs are being established in the Americas. There are public programs, private non-profit programs, private for-profit programs, and those run under the auspices of religious or other charitable groups. Weiss and Mirin list over 100 substance abuse treatment programs in the USA.[20] Substance abuse treatment centers have developed rapidly and now, according to one source, in the USA alone they are more than a three billion dollar per year business.[21]

The approaches vary greatly. One group for teenagers that has approximately 1500 chapters is called 'Toughlove', and they emphasize ' . . . not gentle counseling but harsh confrontations with peers and counsellors: You've acted like a jerk; now you'll grow up'.[22] Other groups take teenage drug addicts and put them through a military-like basic training, giving them discipline, structure, skills, and self-confidence. Still other groups like 'HIS Mansion' in New Hampshire introduce the people who come there for treatment to the disciplined life of a farm, including early rising to milk the cows, hard work, carpentry and other construction skills, and daily Bible study and prayer.

Private live-in programs can cost up to $15,000 per year or more.[23] There is no clear evidence that one approach is vastly superior to another. Over the short run – a year or two – roughly half of those treated remain drug-free. Drug treatment is certainly an area where long term follow-up and careful research needs to be done, but treatment cannot wait until all of the answers are in. There are too many desperate individuals and families who need help. In the meantime, the principles described above may help others plan treatment programs or make better individual choices, should someone in their families need help.

There are no quick fixes in crack treatment. All pharmacological treatments are only adjuncts to the therapeutic process. The medications only assist the patient to re-establish values and relationships. In some ways, the therapeutic process recapitulates child development, in which the child grows in the socializing environment of the family and gradually internalizes the basic values of his or her parents.

ILLUSTRATIVE CASES OF TREATMENT

Examples of successful treatment

Mr A. is a twenty-eight year old married man who worked as a civil servant. He started snorting cocaine five years prior to admission and went on to smoke crack for the past three years. Initially he smoked only sporadically, but eventually he became a daily user, spending approximately $500 per week. His wife, unable to cope with his abuse of her and the neglect of the children, left him. As he became less productive and cooperative at work, his supervisor warned him that he would lose his job unless he sought help. Recognizing that he was losing control of his life, he admitted himself voluntarily to inpatient treatment. Feeling claustrophobic and unable to cope with the structure, he discharged himself and presented himself for assessment at the outpatient clinic. Showing high motivation for treatment, he presented no overt signs of psychopathology and was accepted into the program. Recognising the urgency of his situation vis-à-vis the family and employment, he took his treatment seriously and completed all phases of the program in one year without any relapses. He kept his job throughout the treatment, and, according to his supervisor, his performance improved with the treatment. At about six months into the program, his wife, after attending a number of family sessions, decided to be reconciled with him. He has maintained sobriety for more than 24 months and is functioning well in his family and work life. This case illustrates that the threat of losing a job is a powerful motivation for seeking treatment.

Mr B. is a single thirty year old male from a lower socioeconomic background. He started using marijuana at a very young age and started smoking crack in the early 1980s. Moving into daily use, he lost his job as an entertainer and eventually became a vagrant. Realizing his life had fallen apart, he obeyed the prodding of his sister and was admitted into inpatient treatment, but discharged himself prematurely soon afterwards. Encouraged by a friend who was doing well in the outpatient program, he sought an assessment at the outpatient clinic. On assessment he was depressed but showed no overt signs of cocaine psychosis. He went steadily through the phases of the program with no relapses. In addition to his daily treatment sessions, he faithfully attended Narcotics Anonymous and volunteered at the drug hotline. He has been off crack for four years and is presently working in a halfway house for crack addicts. This case illustrates how a persistent, caring, significant other can be instrumental in helping the most severe crack addict to recover.

Mr C. is a single man who works for an oil company. Working on a ship which went out two to three weeks at a time, he started to smoke crack cocaine three years ago while the ship was in port for three to four weeks at a time. Eventually moving to daily use, he became less interested in his job and often would miss his ship. Recognizing the danger of his addiction, the company mandated that he seek help or lose his job. He was given a leave of absence to seek help at the outpatient clinic. His assessment indicated he was heavily into smoking crack, spending up to $500 per week. Use was particularly heavy on payday. During crack use, he would become passive and give away personal belongings to his drug-using colleagues – for example, he gave away four gold watches in a period of three months. He did extremely well one month into the program, with clean urine and apparent control of cravings. However, on payday (he was paid monthly), the conditioned cues led to severe craving and a return to smoking crack. He returned to the clinic while still feeling cravings and felt he had lost the ability to maintain abstinence. He was given flupenthixol decanoate (10mg) intramuscularly. After three days his cravings subsided, he was less depressed, and he regained his motivation to continue his program. About three days before his next payday, the flupenthixol was repeated and he was able to accept his paycheck with little craving and continue successfully in the program. He has been off crack for ten months, and has returned to his job. During his days in port he attends follow-up group sessions and has urine testing.

This case illustrates the power of cues (here, money) in stimulating craving and leading to relapses, and how they can be helped by flupenthixol.

Ms D. is a thirty-five year old divorced woman who described using drugs since high school. Attractive and industrious, she was able to continue her life uneventfully while using marijuana and alcohol. She started snorting cocaine in the late seventies, but was introduced to crack in the US in 1983. On returning to the Bahamas, she moved into heavy crack smoking in 1984 and 1985. As her frequency and quantity increased, she became less adept at her job and started to neglect her children. She would smoke crack all night and not prepare food for the children. She remembers her son begging her to stop. On one occasion her daughter fell down and hurt her arm. Being high on crack, she ignored the child for three days, only to find when the binge was over that the child's arm was broken.

The awareness of her increasing neglect at home and the threat of losing her job made her seek help. On assessment she was well motivated, determined, and presented no overt psychopathology. She went through the program with no relapses. She has been off cocaine for 5 years and holds an important office job. This case illustrates that the guilt of a mother in not caring for her children can be a motivating factor throughout treatment.

Mr E. is a thirty-three year old married man with a history of drug use. Starting with marijuana and alcohol in high school, he moved on to smoking crack in 1985. He claims that as his crack use increased, he used marijuana less frequently and alcohol more frequently. Moving to daily crack use, he started missing work and performing less effectively on the job. Threatened about losing his job, he enrolled in outpatient cocaine treatment. On assessment he seemed well motivated and had no overt psychopathology. He progressed well in the program for about three months, and then relapsed. He did well for another month, became involved with a woman in the program, and relapsed again. He continued to binge crack. After a series of warnings, he was expelled from the treatment program. After continuing to use crack, he developed pneumonia and was admitted to the hospital. Confronted about inpatient treatment, he begged for another chance. He was allowed to re-enter outpatient treatment. Shortly after re-entering, he was converted at a revival meeting and became intimately involved in a church fellowship. Since then he has gone on to complete the program, and he has been crack-free for eighteen months. His supervisor reports he is doing well on the job. This case illustrates the importance of religious community in the treatment of crack addiction.

Mr F. is a thirty-two year old man with a college degree who has been smoking crack for the past 5 years. After the loss of his job and the break-up of his marriage, he consented to enter an inpatient treatment centre. Completing the total program, he was discharged to a half-way house to prepare to reenter society. After five months of sobriety and working at a regular job, he relapsed and began to smoke crack again. He became haggard and unkempt and became a street vagrant, sleeping in abandoned cars. After lack of income made it difficult to cope with street life, he showed up at a long-term residential treatment program, begging for admission. After the initial screening, he was admitted. He adapted very well to the treatment program, which included spiritual direction (values formation), physical exercise, and vocational training. After a year in the program, he was discharged and is now off crack and working regularly. He has been drug free for 18 months and has had a number of promotions in his job as a salesman. This case demonstrates the need for long term residential programs that provide vocational training.

Examples of unsuccessful treatment

Mr G. is a twenty-four year old man who began using crack cocaine five years ago. Violent and disruptive to his family, he was sent to a long-term treatment centre. Refusing to cooperate with the program, he left and continued to smoke crack. After another threatening episode with his family, he was hospitalized on the cocaine treatment ward of the local state hospital. Suffering intense cravings, he left the program after one month and returned to smoking crack. A year later he became extremely depressed after a crack binge and attempted suicide by cutting an artery. He was admitted to the hospital for treatment of the laceration and was referred to the inpatient cocaine treatment program. Two weeks later he ran away from the hospital and has continued to smoke crack. There might have been a more successful resolution of this case had there been more family involvement in the treatment, or a mandatory patient commitment to an inpatient program.

Mr H. is a forty year old divorced, unemployed man who started snorting cocaine ten years ago and progressed to smoking crack five years ago. Because he was violent and threatening to his ailing widowed mother, she begged the local community mental health centre for help. After much debate and resistance, he consented to enter the inpatient treatment program. However, after an hour on the ward, he angrily walked out, claiming he did not like the rules. In tears the mother begged him to return but he refused and contines to smoke crack cocaine. This patient might have been able to tolerate admission had he been given flupenthixol prior to admission.

References

1. F. H. Gawin and E. H. Ellinwood, 'Cocaine and Other Stimulants: Actions, Abuse, and Treatment', New England Journal of Medicine, 318(18): 1173–82 (1988).
2. Gina Kolata, 'Experts Finding New Hope on Treating Crack Addicts', New York Times, 24 Aug. 1989 (p. 1).
3. Gawin and Ellinwood, op. cit.
4. Kolata, op. cit.
5. Kolata, op.cit.
6. Gawin and Ellinwood, op. cit.
7. R. A. Rawson, J. L. Obert, M. J. McCann, and A. J. Mann, 'Cocaine Treatment Outcome: Cocaine Use Following Inpatient, Outpatient, and No Treatment', National Institute on Drug Abuse Research, Monograph Series 67: 271–7 (1986).
8. Gawin and Ellinwood, op. cit.
9. Remarks by a patient treated in outpatient cocaine treatment at the Community Mental Health Centre, Nassau, Bahamas, 1986.
10. David F. Allen, 'A Model Outpatient Treatment Program for Crack Cocaine Addiction', in preparation.
11. R. D. Weiss, S. M. Mirin, et al., 'Psychopathology in Chronic Cocaine Abusers', American Journal of Drug and Alcohol Abuse 12: 17–29 (1986).
12. F. H. Gawin and H. D. Kleber, 'Abstinence Symptomatology and Psychiatric Diagnosis in Chronic Cocaine Abusers', Archives of General Psychiatry 43: 107–13 (1986).

13. F. H. Gawin, and H. D. Kleber, 'Pharmacological Treatments for Cocaine Abuse', *Psychiatric Clinics of North America* 9: 573–83 (1986).
14. J. F. Jekel, D. F. Allen, H. Podlewski *et al.*, 'Epidemic Cocaine Abuse: Case Study from the Bahamas', *The Lancet* 1: 459–62, 1986.
15. F. H. Gawin, H. D. Kleber, R. Byck *et al.*, 'Desipramine Facilitation of Initial Cocaine Abstinence', *Archives of General Psychiatry* 46: 117–21 (1989).
16. C. A. Dackis and M. D. Gold, 'Bromocriptine as Treatment of Cocaine Abuse', *The Lancet* 1: 151, 1985.
17. F. H. Gawin, D. F. Allen, and B. H. Humblestone, 'Outpatient Treatment of 'Crack' Cocaine Smoking with Flupenthixol Decanoate', *Archives of General Psychiatry* 46: 322–5 (1989).
18. Gawin and Ellinwood, op. cit.
19. G. A. Marlatt and J. R. Gordon, *Relapse Prevention* (New York: Guilford Press, 1985).
20. R. D. Weiss, and S. M. Mirin, *Cocaine* (New York: Ballantine Books, 1987).
21. 'Treatment', *US News & World Report*, 11 September 1989 (p. 74).
22. Ibid.
23. Ibid.

5 Prevention of Crack Abuse

Current therapy for crack abuse is not adequate. Considering only those who present themselves to clinics for treatment, the estimates of the proportion that are helped, through therapy, to maintain a cocaine-free existence for a considerable period of time vary, but most are in the range of 50 per cent.[1] These estimates do not count the unknown but considerable proportion of the crack abusers who never enter treatment. Even for those who have entered treatment, there usually has been several years of progressive stress on the individual and his family until the addict enters treatment. Frequently this stress includes family breakup and lost productivity, the costs of which the addict, his family, and society must bear. For these reasons, crack use should be prevented if at all possible. Knowledge is too inadequate to recommend any single program, but still there is much that can be done now to prevent drug abuse.

POSSIBLE CAUSES OF THE CRACK EPIDEMIC

Do human beings need to alter their psyches?

One school of thought among those who study drug abuse contends that human beings have an inborn need to get 'high', and that society had best put resources into finding a safe, non-addictive, mind-altering or mood-altering drug that can be used to substitute for more dangerous illicit drugs.[2] Prominent among those arguing for this position is Ronald Siegel, a well known research psychopharmacologist. He does admit that current illicit drugs are too dangerous to be used safely. The essence of his argument is that there is an inborn need in human beings to alter their psyches or their states of consciousness from time to time. Others, including William Bennett and Herbert Kleber, the top two US Government Drug Control administrators, are extremely skeptical. In the same article, Dr Kleber was quoted as saying,

I can only note that all previous attempts along this line have ended in disaster. Remember that morphine was used to treat opium addiction, and heroin was used to treat morphine addiction. If the drug Siegel envisions were too good, people would just want more of it.[3]

Pre-existing depression

Research early in the current crack epidemic indicated that a considerable proportion of users in the US had pre-existing depression and appeared to be using the drug to elevate their mood.[4] These users had discovered that cocaine sometimes could have antidepressant effects. The studies suggested that a quarter or more of users in the early 1980s had pre-existing depression, which the users thought was helped by cocaine use. The crack users with mood disorders tended to be able to get off the drug and stay off it when they were given antidepressant medications. However, more recent estimates suggest that the proportion of crack users with pre-existing mood disorders is dropping as the epidemic enlarges.[5]

Other causes of illicit drug abuse

In general it has been found that the more available and inexpensive mind-altering drugs are, the more extensive and intensive will be their use.[6,7] Ultimately the best way to stop the use of drugs is to make them unavailable. However, particularly in the case of crack, the activity of governments so far has had limited effect in reducing the availability of cocaine hydrochloride powder, which is the form imported from South America, and from which crack is made. Interdiction will probably continue to be inadequate without a massive destruction of the coca trees in those areas of the world where they grow well.

On the other hand, even when illicit drugs are freely available, not all persons will use them. The reasons why some persons do and others do not use these drugs are incompletely understood. However, illicit drug use involves increasingly more intense and concentrated experiences, which is consistent with trends in other sensory experiences in industrialized nations. For example, in sweetenings the trend over the past century or more has been toward more refined and concentrated products: instead of natural fruits and vegetables, society has come to prefer foods high in refined cane sugar or even concentrated sweeteners such as saccharin. The same refinement and concentration has occurred with drugs. From smoking opium, abusers have moved to the injection of morphine and heroin, and recently to the highly concentrated designer drugs. Cocaine use has moved from the chewing of coca leaves to the more refined cocaine powder, and now to the devastating coca paste and crack cocaine. In each case, the essential ingredients were refined to provide more intensely concentrated experiences.

Often the desire for pleasure or for new and interesting experiences is a part of the motivation to begin drug use. Also, psychological reasons are found; many of these drugs create, although briefly, the sensation of power, success, attractiveness, potency, or almost anything in which the user feels deficient. An escape into these sensations may be difficult to resist for those who lack a feeling of power and success. Perhaps feelings of powerlessness against the social 'megastructures' of the day – such as big government, industry, unions, etc – contribute to a need to escape through drugs. However, the decision to use illicit drugs has many other precursors, which were discussed in Chapter 3.

PUBLIC HEALTH MODELS OF PREVENTION[8]

A model is a conceptual, mathematical, pictorial, or structural device for enabling human beings to think about the various components of a complex system, and how the parts of the system work together. A conceptual model for the causes of a disease that is commonly used in public health is the triad of *Host – Agent – Environment*. In addition, sometimes it is necessary to add a fourth component to this triad, the *Vector*, when considering diseases carried by insects, arthropods, or other animals, for example. To consider the model, we need to list the factors in the *host* (the person being afflicted by the problem), the specific *agent* causing the problem, and the *environment* and *vector* which, working together, enable the agent to cause its effect.

The Host

Here the Host is the human being who is a potential user of crack. At least between the ages of 15 and 40, most people must be considered potential crack users, if the right opportunity and circumstances occur. Those who feel unsuccessful in their society, or who experience excessive stress, especially males, are at higher risk. Nevertheless, it would be a mistake to assume that any group, successful or not, is free from danger. There may be a general resistance in people with certain characteristics, but that is probably less true for crack than any other illicit drug.

General resistance in the host comes from being basically healthy, mentally and physically. There is evidence that people who are mentally sound and emotionally and spiritually healthy in a supportive environment are less likely to try to use crack, but, in contrast to the situation with infectious diseases, there is no evidence for any specific immunity.

The best protection against experimentation with crack cocaine lies in the knowledge, beliefs, and values of individuals and society. The Health Belief Model may shed some light on how to develop resistance against starting crack use.[9] Those who developed this model studied why persons did or did not seek certain preventive medical interventions, such as immunizations. They described several beliefs that an individual ordinarily must possess before he or she will seek a preventive intervention for himself or his family. Presumably similar beliefs would predict avoidance of health-damaging behaviors.

First, there must be the belief that *the disease or problem is serious* – that is, people must believe that if they use crack, the consequences are likely to be serious for their survival, health, and happiness. Those who have experimented in the past with cocaine powder as a recreational drug and did not have serious adverse effects may have difficulty believing that the new form of cocaine, crack, is really as serious as we maintain. Moreover, as described earlier, until recently even professional opinion reinforced the idea that cocaine is not dangerous. With the developments in the United States since 1987 with crack cocaine, any moderately well informed person is likely to know that it can be dangerous, and the complacent attitudes of the 1970s and early 1980s are rapidly being replaced by belief in the grave danger of cocaine. The tragic deaths of several athletes and other public figures have contributed to this shift in beliefs. The change in beliefs provides new hope that education for cocaine abuse prevention can be effective in the Americas.

A second requirement of the health belief model is that a person must believe that he or she is *susceptible to* – i.e., at risk for – crack abuse. The 'it will never happen to me' syndrome, described by Elkind as the 'personal fable', is commonly found in adolescents and young adults, particularly in males, who need to consider themselves grown up and powerful.[10] The importance of this is suggested by the fact that the very group most subject to the 'personal fable', adolescent and young adult males, is that group most at risk for all drugs, especially cocaine. Convincing young people that they themselves are at risk for addiction if they try crack is probably more difficult than convincing them that crack addiction is bad. The idea that experimentation is too dangerous to try, that one hit of crack might start them on the road to an addictive lifestyle, will probably be the most difficult obstacle. School and other public educational programs should begin early. The best early (and ongoing) education for children, however, is undoubtedly the example set by parents and others who are important to them.

Third, the person must believe that the preventive measure would be *effective* – i.e., that there would be *benefits from the recommended action* (here, avoidance of crack). In this case, it would seem obvious that not using the drug would be a successful prevention of addiction, with clear benefits. It is less obvious that those most at risk will view 'trying' crack – i.e., experimenting with it – as a violation of the non-use principle, which threatens the benefits.

Fourth, the health belief model requires that the recommended action is *not* seen to have *negative consequences* This is problematic for young people and drug abuse, because negative social consequences may be perceived from refusing a drug that is being used by friends and peers. Also, avoidance may be seen as a personal deprivation of intense pleasure. Moreover, in some environments, the avoiding of the crack trade will have negative short-term financial consequences and even may add a risk of bodily harm. Here the model suggests that it is critical to reduce the drug trafficking to a level sufficiently low that avoiding crack is not seen as threatening or disruptive to normal life.

Fifth, the health belief model considers the importance of *cues to action*. Unfortunately, in crack the cues to action are cues to *use the drug* – that is, a treated, recovering addict may be able to get his life back to normal and avoid crack until he is subjected to cocaine cues, usually contacts, experiences, or memories that remind him of pleasurable past experiences with crack. The recovering addict may be unaware of a desire for crack until suddenly the telephone or the door bell rings and the person there is someone he used to smoke crack with, or buy crack from. Such an experience may set off a sudden and overwhelming urge to get and smoke more crack. Indeed, as mentioned in Chapter 3, once the acute phase of addiction is past, the most difficult part of therapy is helping the patient to learn how to deal successfully with these conditioned cues. Certain medications reduce the level of craving for cocaine, but they are not always successful against cues. Unless some method is discovered to turn the positive (attraction) cues into negative (revulsion) cues, the problem of cues to crack will remain.

It is certainly clear that social and psychological factors are critical in the choice of whether or not to use drugs, and in the selection of which drugs to use. Because of the lack of proof that educational strategies alone will be sufficient, we must look beyond the host to the Agent and the Environment of the drug problem.

The Agent

The Agent is crack cocaine. The form of cocaine, and the route of its administration, are absolutely critical for any discussion of the drug to have meaning. The emphasis in this book has been on crack cocaine, although much of the information applies equally well to injecting intravenous cocaine hydrochloride or to smoking coca paste in cigarettes (basuco), which is now becoming available on the world market. The freebase form of cocaine (crack) passes quickly through the lipid membranes of the brain into the central nervous system. As described in Chapter 1, the psychic and addictive effects of cocaine depend on how fast the blood level rises, so here we consider crack as a prototype of those forms of cocaine which cause a very rapid rise, with extreme consequences, including addiction.

Even as the AIDS virus attacks the immune system in such a way as to reduce its capacity to resist infection, crack acts on brain physiology in a way that reduces the ability of the user to resist more cocaine. The user both wants more pleasure, and, when the dysphoric (unpleasant) phase of abuse appears, the user also wants relief. Thus there is both a *push* and a *pull* to use more crack.

The Environment

The environment is another critical element in crack use and abuse. The most important single environmental force is the availability of the drug. Use will be non-existent or limited if the drug is not available or is very expensive. For many, whether they start crack use at all will be determined by whether or not it is available and affordable; if it is not, they may either use no drugs or turn to alternatives.

There is no doubt that the cost of cocaine has dropped considerably over the last few years in terms of the cost per hit or per effective high. This is due to a drop in the cost per unit weight of street cocaine, to an increase in the purity of the drug (so that less is required for a good hit), and to the switch from snorting powder to inhaling crack. The latter gives more pleasurable effect per weight than does snorting, so less is needed per hit. By clever marketing, a powerful hit is now available in the US for $5–10.

The external pressures to buy crack, to participate in trafficking, and to avoid fighting against the pushers in order to be safe, are greater than for any previous illicit drug. The crack sales force is far more extensive and decentralized than for most other drugs, which means that modern marketing methods are going beyond the product to the sales organization as well. It takes a massive and dependable supply system to provide over $100 billion of powdered cocaine per year just to the United States, so that the providers, the wholesalers, and the retailers all can make a good profit from the drug.

The fear of AIDS from needles is another factor in the environment that is encouraging users to switch from intravenous drugs, including heroin and cocaine, to crack. This is ironic, because in the United States at least, frequently crack abusers will begin prostitution to obtain money for the drug, and this produces a direct increase in the risk of AIDS. Also, prostitution increases the chances of various sexually transmitted diseases which, in turn, increase the chance of acquiring AIDS through sexual intercourse, because the virus of AIDS can more readily enter the body through mucous membranes that have ulcers or are inflamed from sexually transmitted disease.

The Vector

The Vector is the drug trafficking system, including the local pushers. A debate continues as to how effective arresting and incarcerating pushers will be in the drug war, just as debate continues as to the role of mosquito control in the eradication of malaria. Crack is unusual in that the agent itself stimulates the replication of the vector, the pusher. It is also similar to many insect-borne diseases, in that the agent undergoes a necessary change while in (the possession of) the vector: the conversion from cocaine powder to crack. Logic would dictate, however, that by one method or another, the retail source must be eliminated or reduced if a crack prevention and control effort is to be effective.

LEVELS OF PREVENTION

Primary prevention

One of the most used public health models for conceptualizing control options is called the 'levels of prevention'.[11] Primary prevention consists of methods to prevent the development of the disease-forming process, so that it never really gets a start. Primary prevention includes two related kinds of efforts, the first of which is called 'health promotion' and the second 'specific protection'.

Health promotion refers to general efforts to improve the nutrition, the environment, and the health knowledge and behavior of individuals and a community, so as to promote good health. *Specific protection* refers to targeted, usually technologic efforts to prevent specific diseases. The classic example of specific protection is immunization against infectious diseases. Fluoridation of the water supply to reduce dental caries and the addition of specific vitamins and minerals to foods to prevent certain nutritional diseases are other examples.

Primary prevention includes measures to eliminate crack from the environment, or at least to reduce its prevalence and increase its cost. The panoply of methods to accomplish this include drug interdiction, prevention of money laundering, legal enforcement within a country, drug testing, etc. Educational efforts to increase the resistance of people to initiating crack use would also be primary prevention, and the effect would be somewhat like immunization. Educational efforts against cigarette smoking have had, at best, modest success; it remains to be seen whether the same will be true for education against crack use. If education is to work, it should begin early and address elements of the health belief model.

One important idea from infectious disease epidemiology, which comes from the immunization principle, is the contrast between 'individual immunity' and 'herd immunity'. A vaccine, such as that against tetanus, can confer the immunized individual considerable protection, but the individual's immunity contributes nothing to the protection of anyone else. Other vaccines, which not only prevent the immunized individual from becoming ill but also reduce his ability to spread a germ to someone else, are said to confer 'herd immunity'. That is, when most of the people in the 'herd' are resistant to a dangerous virus, they in turn protect non-immune individuals.

It is to be hoped that there is an equivalent of 'herd immunity' in crack abuse, possibly citizens who, realizing the danger of the drug, not only refuse it for themselves (individual immunity) but also work as families and neighborhoods to rid their areas of drug dealers and so protect the innocent. The only infectious disease known to have been eradicated is smallpox. Its eradication was possible more due to the ability of smallpox vaccine to confer herd immunity than to the individual immunity it also provided. The same may be true for crack, and it may be the way societies gradually become resistant to a new danger.

Other useful approaches include teaching children how to 'say no', and helping them to clarify their own values.[12] The spiritual issues, such as meaning and purpose in life, should not be avoided.[13] The efforts of Christians and Muslims to build positive alternatives to drugs in the neighborhoods, such as sports, counseling, educational programs, and art and craft programs, are health-promoting activities that will have effects far beyond the prevention of crack abuse.[14]

The home environment, including the pattern of control and nurturing of children, appears to be important in drug abuse. As reported in *Science News*, an ongoing study that identified different patterns of childrearing found that:

> Parents who consistently set down clear standards for conduct and offer freedom within specific limits produce teenagers who perform better on academic tests, are more emotionally and socially stable, and use alcohol and illicit drugs substantially less than youngsters from other types of families.[15]

Secondary prevention

Secondary prevention implies the early detection of a problem before it has become symptomatic, and then providing the necessary-sary treatment to prevent negative consequences. Medically this usually implies screening for disease, making a careful diagnosis on the persons who screen positive, and treating those who are diseased, with the hope of a cure (in cancer or syphilis) or of preventing complications (in high blood pressure).

There are ways of screening for crack use, such as doing chemical analyses on the urine. Increasingly this is being used in sports and in some critical jobs, such as air traffic controllers, but it raises questions of freedom of the individual. In general, it seems unlikely that ordinary citizens will be subjected to random screening before some negative event (such as an automobile accident), but people in sensitive jobs, especially transportation, may increasingly be screened. Technically the goal of this kind of screening is more to protect society from drug-induced incompetence (i.e. primary prevention of injury) than for the welfare of the individual screened (secondary prevention.)

Some psychiatrists have claimed that the earlier in the progression of an addiction the patient begins treatment, the better the outcome is likely to be.[16] This would seem to make sense, but it is possible that self-selection also plays a role – i.e., the earlier a person comes for treatment, the more concerned and motivated he may be. Certainly it is easier for a crack abuser to return to his normal life if he has not pilfered goods or injured other persons while using crack. This may justify screening efforts in the eyes of some people, but large scale random screening of individuals for cocaine and other drugs is likely to meet with strong opposition from those concerned with civil rights issues, as well as from those concerned about the cost and practicality of drug screening programs.

Tertiary prevention

Tertiary prevention means the medical and public efforts that occur after a problem has become evident in an individual or community. The goal here is to prevent as many negative effects of the disease or problem as possible by treatment and rehabilitation, so that individuals can return as soon a possible to maximum social functioning. Treatment and rehabilitation have been discussed in Chapter 4.

These public health models are useful for categorizing options and for checking specific programs against them, so as to avoid gaps. They do not provide magic solutions. However they can help us to analyze what our options are and what research and programs need to be carried out, so we may channel our efforts efficiently and effectively.

WHAT CAN BE DONE?

Much of the research on the causes and prevention of drug abuse was done prior to the current crisis in crack cocaine. Therefore, the extent to which the previous insights can be transferred to crack abuse is unclear. Recent research suggests that crack addiction is more likely to occur after one use of crack than with a single trial with any other drug, so that trying crack is especially dangerous. For some, experimenting with crack may be like experimenting with jumping off a cliff. Although the proportion of people who try crack who become addicted to it is not certain, the danger of experimentation is not in doubt.

Socioeconomic differences are less crucial in determining the likelihood of crack abuse, except that low income neighborhoods are more likely to be 'taken over' by the drug forces than are higher income areas. The social environment, including the prevailing general attitude toward drug use, and the extent of that use among friends, is clearly a critical element.

If the social environment is an important source of initiating cocaine use, it is likely that it will be an important factor in the prevention of its use as well. The 1989 national Gallup poll in the US reported not only that the drug situation was the top national concern, but also that about three-fourths of teenagers and about one-half of adults want to volunteer to fight the drug.

Responses to the poll suggest that the attitudes toward crack, and the solutions being proposed by individuals, increasingly reflect a 'war mentality'. It is possible that this is a useful mentality for a society to have regarding crack abuse. Such an outlook may not be as effective against other illicit drugs, where the safety or ethics of use, or the social impact of the drug, are less clear. Such a mentality, however, makes it easier to identify friends and foes, determine one's own obligations, feel part of an important social enterprise, commit social resources, and limit some individual freedoms. There is even a chance to become a *bona fide* hero, through leadership and public recognition. The importance of the social environment appears to be confirmed by the profound negative impact which results from drug traffic taking over a neighborhood, and the early apparently positive effects of isolated cases where neighborhoods united to, in effect, 'throw the bums out', usually with special help from police.

The war analogy is being seen more often in newspapers[17] and magazines.[18] The increasing number of persons being shot due to wars between drug gangs[19] or because a person was trying to fight against an invasion of the neighborhood by drug traffickers, lends credence to the terminology.

Ministers in US black communities, both Christian and Muslim, have organized community activities for young people after school, such as education, recreation, tutorials, and employment assistance.[20] To show the community commitment, marches and rallies against drugs are becoming common. In addition to using education, black Muslims have established large patrol groups that do not use violence but do use walkie-talkies and manage gradually to convince drug traffickers that they would be best off moving elsewhere. One black Muslim leader was quoted as saying 'Black men have got to have faith in whatever God they believe in and take a stand. That's what we're doing'.[21]

In Kansas City, Missouri, a very wealthy industrialist, Ewing Marion Kauffman, has a program called Project Choice, to provide financial support to a large number of inner-city young people to enable them to go to college or even graduate school.[22] His support is contingent on their remaining drug and pregnancy free and maintaining good grades until graduation. He also has supported a drug abuse prevention program called 'Project STAR (Students Taught Awareness and Resistance) to enable high school students to learn how to resist the pressures toward drug use.

To date most of the success stories for individual recovery from crack abuse, or of recovery of an area from the problem, appear to combine a turning or returning to fundamental values, including religion, and a supportive community. Regarding the role of religion in prevention, Arterburn and Burns see an important contradiction:

> It's rare to find God mentioned in secular discussion on how to prevent alcohol or other drug problems. That God is left out of *prevention* materials is ironic, as mention of Him saturates the literature on *treatment*.[23]

Sometimes action by law enforcement agencies is an important part of the solution. Police action, however, is usually not adequate alone. The community must be sufficiently committed to ridding themselves of the cocaine problem that they are willing to take some risks in the effort.

References

1. 'Hour by Hour: Crack', *Newsweek*, 28 Nov. 1988, p. 77.
2. J. Beaty, 'Do Humans Need to Get High?' *Time*, 21 Aug. 1989.
3. Ibid.
4. F. H. Gawin and H. D. Kleber, 'Abstinence symptomatology and psychiatric diagnosis in chronic cocaine users', *Archives of General Psychiatry* 43: 107–13, 1986.
5. R. D. Weiss, S. M. Mirin, *et al.*, 'Psychopathology in cocaine abusers. Changing trends', *Journal of Nervous and Mental Diseases*, 176(12): 719–25 (1988).
6. R. Byck, Testimony before the Select Committee on Narcotics Abuse and Control, House of Representatives, Ninety-sixth Congress, July 24, 26, and October 10, 1979.
7. 'Arrests Skyrocketing as Drug Prices Tumble', *New Haven Register*, 13 Dec. 1988 (p. 6).
8. Adapted from: J. F. Jekel, 'Public health approaches to the cocaine problem', in D. F. Allen, ed., *The Cocaine Crisis* (1987), pp. 107ff.
9. I. M. Rosenstock, 'What research in motivation suggests for public health', *American Journal of Public Health* 50(2): 295–302 (March 1960).
10. D. Elkind, *The Child and Society* (New York: Oxford University Press, 1979).
11. J. Mausner and S. Kramer, *Epidemiology: An Introductory Text*, 2nd Edn (Philadelphia: W. B. Saunders, 1985).
12. J. F. Toohey, 'Activities for the Clarification of Values in Drug and Substance Abuse Education: A Manual for the Instructor', (Tempe, AZ: Arizona State University, 1985)
13. V. Frankl, *Man's Search for Meaning* (New York: Washington Square Press, 1963)
14. 'Ministers Mobilize Against the Death of a Race', *Ebony Magazine* August 1989, 160–4.
15. B. Bower, 'Teenagers reap broad benefits from 'authoritative' parents', *Science News* 136: 117, 19 August 1989.
16. M. Neville, 'Treatment issues, medical and criminal perspectives in the realities of the provision of treatment to cocaine addicts in the Bahamas', presented at the International Drug Symposium,

Nassau, Bahamas, 20–22 November 1985.
17. L. Eardley, 'US Official: Drug War Looms Here', *St. Louis Post Dispatch*, Saturday, Aug. 5, 1989 (p. 1).
18. 'War: The Drug Crisis', *Ebony Magazine*, Aug. 1989, special issue.
19. G. Hackett and M. A. Lerner, 'L.A. Law: Gangs and Crack', *Newsweek Magazine*, April 27, 1989.
20. 'The Muslims to the Rescue', *Ebony Magazine*, Aug. 1989, special issues (136–40).
21. Ibid.
22. D. Narine, 'The Billionaire and the Students', *Ebony Magazine*, August 1989, special issue, pp. 146–50.
23. S. Arterburn and J. Burns, 'Drug-Proof your kids', *Focus on the Family*, Oct. 1989, p. 3.

6 The Societal Challenge of Crack Addiction

Crack cocaine has had devastating effects at three levels of society:

1. Individual addicts and their families;
2. Poor urban neighborhoods in big cities; and
3. The authority and order of entire cities and nations.

INDIVIDUALS AND FAMILIES

The first danger is damage, sometimes beyond repair, to the lives of individual crack addicts and their families. This effect knows no socioeconomic boundaries. Many will recall the sudden deaths of several well known athletes (e.g., basketball player Len Bias and American football players Johnny Rogers, Larry Bethea, and David Croudip). Cocaine has been related to the deaths of famous persons – including the son of a former US Senator and some well-known entertainment figures (e.g., John Belushi). Equally well publicized was the apparently cocaine-related behavior of 47-year-old lawyer, Joel Steinberg, who was convicted of beating his common-law wife, Hedda Nussbaum, and of fatally beating his six year old adopted daughter, Lisa Steinberg.[1]

Already there is evidence of crack appearing in Britain; for example, in Nottinghamshire 113 vials of crack recently were seized.[2] The cocaine supply mostly comes from Colombia, South America, and appears to enter Europe through Spain. The only crack use reported from Germany so far has been in American troops, but pure powdered cocaine is widely available in Europe, where the price has been falling.[3]

POOR NEIGHBORHOODS

Crack has produced the most powerful drug culture yet known in lower socioeconomic areas, turning poor neighborhoods into combat zones controlled by the forces financed by cocaine. *Time* put it this way:

> They hang out in parking lots and playgrounds. They commandeer vacant apartments. In some cities they have become occupying armies, besieging entire housing complexes. They are the drug dealers who have terrorized public housing projects since the birth of the crack-cocaine trade.[4]

The structure and functioning of families who live in these areas often are damaged beyond repair.[5,6] Crack has become, as suggested by *Time* magazine the newest US 'jobs program' for inner-city children.[7] Whether or not the children involved in the crack trade are in gangs, they often become the primary money-winners in the family, take over the power role in the family, and may even strengthen this role by making their parents crack addicts, although whether this activity is a conscious strategy for the aggrandizement of family power is doubtful.[8] This kind of danger could happen in other industrialized nations where there are concentrated areas of urban underemployment and poor housing.

SOCIAL ORDER AND LEGAL AUTHORITY

The social values and legal authority of entire societies are being undermined, either directly by armed action, or by the rot of corruption from within. Considerable 'police power' (the power to regulate the life and behavior of citizens) is being exercised by powerful and well-armed drug gangs, particularly in Los Angeles, California, and Washington DC.[9] They have mounted a strong challenge to the ability of police to prevent near-anarchy conditions in many areas of these cities.

In the producer nations (especially Colombia) the drug forces have developed a separate military power within the nation so strong that it challenges the national government, including the military, in its strength and hegemony. The most obvious example is in the nation of Colombia, where the cocaine cartels – a loose association of drug lords that control an estimated 80 per cent of the cocaine entering the US[10] – control much of the countryside. One of the biggest cities, Medellin, is terrorized and largely controlled

by cocaine forces.[11] More than 3000 persons were murdered in
Medellin in 1988, about 5 times the murder rate in New York for
that year. In August 1989, three assassinations occurred, which, in
effect, announced all-out war between the cocaine forces and the
Colombian government. Killed were the police chief of Medellin,
a candidate for President of the Country, and a judge who had
pronounced sentence on a drug baron.[12] The President of Colombia
announced a return to a policy of immediate extradition of drug
leaders to the US, but a similar attempt in the past produced so
strong a wave of violence from the drug forces that it was cancelled.
President Vargas said that the survival of Colombian society was at
stake.[13]

At first, the local people in Medellin were not too worried about
the cocaine traffic:

> They were getting rich off the gringos, 'an entirely respectable
> way for a Latin to accumulate wealth', says Maria Alves Osorio,
> a middle-class mother of three who is now alarmed at Medel-
> lin's lawlessness. 'Our children weren't taking cocaine, so every-
> thing was fine'. Many residents welcomed the money that drugs
> brought to the city and the jobs they created . . . [14]

Moreover, in Colombia the local drug godfathers become philan-
thropists, helping poor people and doing 'good works' in the area,
so that any attempt to remove them results in local opposition.
However, the nation of Colombia and the city of Medellin soon
began to be invaded by 'basuco,' a cheap version of coca paste, and
addicts began to develop in large numbers. The drug cartel could
not resist the profit of selling the unused coca paste that was left
over from the manufacturing process, so the people of Colombia,
themselves, also are now paying a price for having the drug cartels
based in their country. Also, it has recently been discovered that
the middle class in Colombia has started to use crack heavily.[15]

Healy described how cocaine has complicated the plight of one of
the poorest of South American nations, Bolivia.[16] During the current
severe economic crisis, cocaine has provided employment for tens
of thousands of poor families and traders and has produced bad-
ly-needed foreign exchange. At the same time, cocaine has brought
many problems, such as corruption, drug abuse, and decreased
food production. There is strong opposition from 'well organized
peasant unions' to eradication of coca production . The tension

appears to be economic survival versus societal well-being.

Other nations are taking severe legal steps to counteract the drug traffic. Iran and Indonesia, both Muslim nations, put drug traffickers to death. In Cuba, national hero General Arnaldo Ochoa Sanchez was sentenced to death for dealing in drugs.[17] This severe approach, at least for the near future, may be possible only in totalitarian or semi-totalitarian states; the challenge to the free West is how to control drugs without resorting to such extreme measures.

Nobody expects the drug forces to mount a major military challenge to the established government of Western nations with strong defense forces, but many third world nations without large defense forces are becoming increasingly concerned. The prime minister of one such country, Jamaica, recommended that the United Nations develop an anti-drug strike force, because the drug forces act internationally in a planned, coordinated way. Drug gangs that challenge *local* police power do operate in areas of the US, and, therefore, presumably they could operate in other free societies, despite the presence of strong national defense forces[18]

Corruption

In every country where there is major cocaine traffic, large amounts of cocaine money are used to buy the cooperation of government, police, and business persons.[19,20] The susceptibility of a nation to this danger is related to many factors, including the equity with which national resources are distributed and the prevailing value systems of the country. No nation should consider itself immune to the immense bribes that the cocaine forces are able and willing to make.

SHOULD CRACK SALE AND USE BE LEGALIZED?

In the US some voices now argue that the current problem with crack is largely the result of its being an illegal drug, creating an entire illicit production, transport, and distribution system that limits an enormously profitable field to those who break the law. This, in turn, it is argued, encourages the spread of crack use. They believe that if illegal profits were removed from the picture, it would weaken drug cartels, reduce the local pressure for sales of the drug, and lower the price of the drug, thereby decreasing the pressure to steal to obtain drug money.[21-23]

There are prominent supporters of legalizing drugs. Kurt Schmoke, Mayor of Baltimore and a former prosecutor, claims that the current policies – which keep cocaine illegal – are a failure.[24] Nobel Prize-winning economist, Milton Friedman, was quoted as saying 'The harm that is done by drugs is predominantly caused by the fact that they are illegal. You would not have had the crack epidemic if it was [sic] legal'.[25] As *Time* magazine stated, 'The bottom line for those favoring legalization: drug-related crime damages society far more than drug usage itself'.[26] The model that they point to is alcohol, and the presumed failure of Prohibition in the 1930s.

A contrary view

The authors of this book are opposed to the legalizing of cocaine and crack, which, in our judgment, is a proposal not based on good scientific evidence, nor on an appreciation of the addictive danger of crack or of the marketing creativity of those in the drug trade.[27] How would legalization reduce the pressures to sell crack? Most of the pushers are addicts themselves, and legalizing the drug would mean that selling crack is a safe, legal 'profession'. Pushers would still have the profit motive to sell drugs, just as people and companies have the profit motive to sell hamburgers or liquor (in the US), fish and chips or bitter (in the UK), or beer (in Germany). Legitimate organizations might compete with existing cocaine cartels to produce and market cocaine, producing conflict, or the cartels might become legitimate 'sole source' suppliers of cocaine to many distribution companies. The biggest difference would be, it is argued, that the cost of the drug would drop considerably from its present low, and there would need to be less crime to pay for the drug. However, the lower price also would make it easier for people to get started on crack. Plentiful crack, and, hence a lower price, does not mean lack of crime. In fact, an abundance of cocaine caused a battle between the Medellin and Cali (Colombia) cocaine cartels. The Medellin cartel had previously avoided the New York cocaine market by agreement, but reneged when cocaine became more plentiful.[28] There were many deaths, both in Colombia and New York, as different groups struggled to control the 'market'.[29] There is no reason to believe that if selling the drug became legal, there would no longer be deadly competition between cartels, rings, and gangs. The various Mafia families fight to control legal, as well as illegal markets. As expressed by Engelsman, 'It is unrealistic to assume that with legalization international criminal organizations would terminate their illegal practices, at least in the short term'.[30]

It is known that the cheaper a psychoactive drug is, the greater the frequency and quantity with which it will be used.[31–32] If legalization were to lower the price of crack considerably, there would be a temporary or permanent increase in use and addiction. Crack is *already* cheap per 'hit'. Most users become addicted and enter into a lifestyle in which nothing but cocaine matters; their drug habit overwhelms everything else in their lives.

The process of becoming addicted to crack is not so expensive now that it ordinarily requires crime. The initial crack use by a future addict is often funded out of his own resources. Eventually, however, the cocaine lifestyle cripples job performance and home life; desperation and crime begin. Lowering the price of crack would increase experimentation and start more young people on a career of crack use, thus ultimately increasing, rather than reducing, the social impact of the drug.

A few who are extremely wealthy may not have to worry about job performance or the money needed for cocaine; they may be able to use crack until they die or lose interest, but this does not describe most people in this world. Whether a week's crack costs $100 or $1000, eventually there will be devastation to every abuser's social functioning, and this will damage society whether or not the crack purchased is legal.

We do not minimize the importance of the debate that Mayor Schmoke and others are advancing. Certainly we agree with Mr. Schmoke that ' . . . we can't prosecute our way out of this situation'.[33] One reason a law enforcement approach *alone* is inadequate is that it rapidly produces overloaded courts, overcrowded prisons, and a paralyzed judicial system that is forced to release arrested persons with all but the most severe drug-related offenses.[34–36] We do not contend that prosecution is the only, or even the primary, tool for controlling the cocaine problem. And it would appear to be prudent to make a distinction between non-pusher users and those who attempt to market the drug, in terms of the severity of sentencing.

If crack is an incredibly dangerous, deadly, and socially corrosive drug, then, based on the evidence we have reviewed and experienced, legalization would send the wrong message to the citizens of a nation. Legalization would say either that the drug is fundamentally safe, or that the government has washed its hands of the problem and left people to deal with it without government support. Neighborhoods that are being destroyed could not count on assistance from police to help them to clear their area of drug pushers. Drug educators would be in the untenable position of saying 'this drug is terribly dangerous and you should not even get started on it, but I have to tell you that its use is perfectly legal'. It is doubtful that railroad engineers, airplane pilots, and air traffic controllers, and many others whose consistent and accurate work we rely on, could be kept from 'recreational use' of a legal drug. Wilson published an excellent essay on the dangers of legalizing cocaine in *Commentary* where he analyzes parallels with the situation historically with heroin and other drugs.[37]

One reason so many people were caught off guard by the crack epidemic is that, on the basis of prior experience with cocaine powder, they thought they knew cocaine and how to control it. They were not easily convinced that crack cocaine was very different from snorted cocaine powder, and therefore, that a big problem existed. As the evidence of crack cocaine's danger becomes overwhelming, attitudes are changing and there is some stiffening of the national resolve in the countries most heavily involved. However, the response has taken so long to develop that the enemy has become deeply entrenched and well organized, and will now be vastly more difficult to eliminate.

A NATIONAL RESPONSE

It is clear to us that there is no adequate *single* approach to the problem of dangerous, illicit drugs, especially to crack cocaine. Policies must be balanced, with a strong national commitment. A central question is whether the crack problem is primarily 'demand-driven' or 'provider-driven'.[38] In one sense this question is moot, because once a person has gotten a good start on crack or intravenous cocaine, it most certainly *is* demand driven. Crack is perhaps the most strongly self-reinforcing drug known.[39] Engelsman stated '. . . demand and supply are not two separate worlds, but are closely related'.[40] The issue is whether demand can be stopped before people start using it at all. An unfettered sales force would make it that much easier for children and adults alike to try free samples.

Just as it is not realistic to expect that the crack problem can be solved just by law enforcement, neither is it realistic to expect that it can be solved by education alone. It has been reported that many programs find they can improve knowledge and information, but that the improved knowledge did not usually produce major changes in either attitudes toward drugs or drug use practices.[41]

Information alone should be seen not primarily as a mass policy tool but as a way to give *individual persons* – children and adults alike – sufficient information so they can make informed choices. At least those who are already predisposed to altering their psychic environment with drugs can be helped to know the danger they face with crack. We expect that good education will cause some reduction in the amount of experimentation with cocaine, but that should be seen as a secondary benefit. The analogy is to family planning, which is a method to enable *individuals and families* to make choices regarding their fertility. Family planning is not a method of population control, because it is based on the desires of individual families and not the policy makers, although the net effect may be somewhat similar. Likewise the goal of education is to enable each individual in a society to make an informed, high quality choice, not to impose a particular social policy, however wise that might be.

A further benefit of education might be an increased support by the electorate for a governmental and societal commitment against crack. Lack of knowledge and general concern led to an underestimation of the dangers of cocaine in the US in the early and mid-1980s, for which ignorance the US is now paying dearly.

The educational message

The foundation of a national response is an *informed* citizenry, which understands clearly the special dangers of crack use and the reasons for not beginning its use. This educational effort, as with AIDS, must begin in early childhood, be continued by home, school, and church during school age, and be reinforced thereafter. The content should not just say that cocaine is dangerous, but it must give reasons and deal with fundamental values and rights, so that students and citizens consider the implications for their future, and that of their nation, when they decide to alter their state of consciousness. The idea that crack users are 'messing with their brains' is an important one to get across, especially to young people, whatever the way it is presented.

Information about crack and other drugs should be honest and realistic, or it will not be believed. It would be folly to deny that crack can be extremely pleasurable. Pushers would need only to persuade an individual to try a 'hit' – even free of charge – to prove that the educators were either ignorant about the subject, or deliberately misleading their audience.

Those providing the information, especially parents, must believe what they are saying and live accordingly. The hypocrisy of drug-using parents telling children not to use drugs is obvious, and its effect is likely to be the reverse of what is intended. Moreover, an honest educational effort about the evils of any drug will be weakened or destroyed if the drugs of concern are legalized.

Values

Crack has an unrivaled ability to unmask the true values of a society. Nations must clarify their own *values* and act accordingly. If a society professes to be concerned with the poor, and insists there are better alternatives to their plight than drugs, the total range of social responses to unemployment and poverty must affirm those stated values. If pleasure is a dominant value of a society, it will be difficult to convince its citizens that drugs have no proper place.

Central to the values of a society are its religious beliefs and commitments. The best and most permanent conversions *from* crack and other drugs usually are conversions *to* something, or someone, else. If individual persons, and their society, have few meaningful commitments beyond self-indulgence, they are ripe for harvesting by the forces of psychoactive drugs. It is the family, neighborhood, city, and nation that is *committed* to something beyond itself that will succeed in giving its members the courage to resist dangers from within despite a possible risk to life.

Moreover, family, neighborhoods, and churches are 'mediating structures' to help individuals resist the huge, powerful 'mega-structures' of society.[42] These must become 'activated', turned on to mutual commitment and to values beyond themselves, if we are to find the power to resist the drug forces.

The use of force

Organized *intimidation* whether by neighborhood traffickers, youth gangs or others, must be dealt with by the police forces quickly and effectively, *before* these groups can become well entrenched. A fast response requires appropriate ongoing surveillance for drug trafficking, on an area-by-area basis. The honest people in every community badly need to know that their concerns will be heard and that they can depend upon a quick response. Part of the problem in the US was the badly delayed response of its population, including the government, to reports of the growing cocaine threat in the early 1980s.

Laundering of drug money

One difficulty with popular discussion of the use of police power to fight cocaine is the assumption that one is referring only to arresting pushers and users of the drug. In fact, some of the most useful legal techniques do not deal with individuals but with the *system* that makes trafficking possible.

For example, it is more difficult for the drug system to hide and transport the paper money they receive than the cocaine itself! As expressed by *Time* magazine, 'Behind every successful drug syndicate lies a complex mechanism for recycling bundles of tainted cash into respectable assets'.[43] This is called 'laundering' or 'green-washing' the money.

Until recently, Switzerland was the primary country in Europe where this was done (although the majority of the money apparently came from sales of heroin rather than cocaine). The disclosure of money laundering in Switzerland caused an international furore and a Swiss political scandal.[44,45] Now the country is tightening its laws and procedures regarding large deposits, both to restore its international reputation and because the drugs have come into the nation along with the money for laundering: 'Switzerland has one of the highest heroin-addiction rates in Europe . . . ' quoted *Newsweek* magazine.[46] Although nobody is sure how much money leaves the US each year because of the drug trade, it probably rivals the current balance of payments deficit due to all other economic exchange. The implications of this for the economic viability of a heavy cocaine-importing nation are not certain, but they are serious.

INTERNATIONAL EFFORTS

June 1988 began a year of rapid developments in limiting the international flow of drug money, when the annual economic summit in Toronto of the leaders of the US, Britain, Canada, France, West Germany, Italy, Japan, and the European Community called for a new international task force against drugs.[47] Their declaration stated, in part:

> The illegal use of drugs and illicit trafficking in them poses grave risks to the peoples of summit countries as well as the peoples of source and transit countries . . . The complexity of the problem requires additional international cooperation, in particular to trace, freeze and confiscate the proceeds of drug traffickers, and to curb money laundering.

In October 1988, the Luxembourg-based Bank of Credit and Commerce International was implicated in a major money-laundering scheme, and seven of its bankers arrested in the US after being lured there. The bank had laundered $14 million dollars for the US Customs service narcotic agents, and undoubtedly much more for the real drug cartels, which includes the Colombian cartel based in Medellin.[48] *Time* magazine went on to say, 'Within 72 hours after the Tampa trap was sprung, American and British customs agents arrested 40 bankers and narcotics traffickers in London and several US cities on money laundering and other charges'.[49]

In December 1988, 43 countries signed a new United Nations convention that will enable these countries to 'freeze and confiscate bank accounts and extradite suspects'.[50] In March 1989 the US Government indicted 127 people in another extensive drug money-laundering scheme.[51]

Increasingly, laws are needed to limit the size of cash deposits, both at one point in time and over extended periods of time, and to require documentation of the source of the bills. Such laws are coming into use and are making the money-changing aspect of the drug trade increasingly problematic. In addition, laws against the manufacture, import, sales, and possession of drug paraphernalia, such as water pipes and plastic 'crack' vials, provide possible techniques to limit the speed with which expansion of drug traffic can occur. Now drug paraphernalia are openly marketed through mail-order catalogs in the US.

Another international dimension of the crack problem is international friction and the possibility of a concerned user nation mounting military efforts against the producers, manufacturers, or transporters of cocaine. Already the US has participated in a joint military expedition against drug manufacture in one South American nation. As one of the Colombian drug lords, Carlos Lehder Rivas, expressed it, 'Cocaine is the Third World's atomic bomb'.[52]

FUTURE DRUG PROBLEMS: ICE

This book has focused on crack cocaine abuse, because it is the most serious world-wide drug problem at this time. Without doubt, however, other drugs will replace cocaine as the worst drug scourge sooner or later. In an article published in 1986, we warned that the combination of kitchen laboratories making designer drugs, and modern marketing methods to sell them, boded ill for the future.[53]

Already there is in existence a new designer drug that may replace crack cocaine in a few years as the leading worldwide drug problem. It is a crystalline, smokable form of methamphetamine ('speed'), which is called 'ice' in the street.[54] Its psychic effect is quite similar to that of crack cocaine, except that the high lasts for several hours, even up to a day, instead of perhaps 15 minutes with crack. As one drug worker in Honolulu (where it has become popular) put it, 'They think it is a drug from heaven because of the long high'.[55]

Another difference between crack and 'ice' is that for 'ice', the crash, if anything, is even worse. Another drug worker in Honolulu said, 'They go absolutely crazy. They are bouncing off the walls'.[56]

There is much experimentation going on in illicit laboratories, and many new designer drugs and drug combinations are being developed. Some may ultimately prove more dangerous and difficult to control that either crack cocaine or 'ice'. Those familiar with 'ice' have predicted it will become the leading drug problem of the 1990s, but others believe that the drug's side effects are unpleasant enough that this will not happen.

Crack is at least a good paradigm for planning to resist future, as well as present, drug problems. Ultimately it may prove more difficult to eliminate drugs that can be made in home chemistry laboratories, like ice, than those which are imported, like cocaine and heroin.

Crack cocaine almost certainly prepares a society for the use of 'ice', because it also is smoked to get an extreme high, and the short time for each high gets frustrating to the crack user. If 'ice' begins to challenge crack cocaine for domination of the drug market, we may see turf wars between those pushing crack and those pushing 'ice'. On the other hand, 'ice' might cause the bottom to drop out of the world market for cocaine, causing major economic problems for those countries whose economies depend heavily on the growing, manufacture, and/or shipping of cocaine.

The implications of this look into the future are: (1) our education efforts must concern drug use in general, and not be limited to cocaine, and (2) we cannot put all our trust in creating barriers to drugs at our borders, because the source of the next drug threat may well be laboratories in our own nations.

Defeating the drug problem will takes the same kind of anticipation, preparedness, and national will that was required to win World War II. We hope Europe will use these errors to avoid the dangers of appeasement and lack of preparedness in this war.

References

1. R. D. McFadden, 'Conviction Indicated Intent', *New York Times*, 31 Jan. 1989 (p. B5).
2. C. R. Whitney, 'Crack Use Starts in Fearful Europe', *New York Times* 27 July 1989.
3. Ibid.
4. 'Evicting the Drug Dealers', *Time*, 1 May 1989 (p. 41).
5. G. Kolata, 'In Cities, Poor Families Are Dying of Crack', *New York Times*, 11 Aug. 1989.
6. J. V. Lamar, 'Kids Who Sell Crack', *Time*, 9 May 1988 (pp. 20–33).
7. Ibid.
8. Kolata, op. cit.
9. T. Morganthau *et al.*, 'The Drug Gangs', *Newsweek*, 28 March 1988 (pp. 20–9).
10. J. Borrell, 'The Most Dangerous City', *Time*, 21 March 1988 (pp. 45–6).
11. Ibid.

12. 'In Wake of Latest Slaying, Colombia Will Seek to Extradite Drug Figures', *New York Times*, 20 Aug. 1989 (p. 12).
13. Ibid.
14. Borrell, op. cit.
15. J. B. Treaster, 'Columbia Strains to Stem Rampant Cocaine Abuse', *New York Times*, 15 Sept. 1989, p. 1.
16. K. Healy, 'Bolivia and Cocaine: A Developing Country's Dilemmas', *British Journal of Addictions* 83: 19–23 (1988).
17. M. A. Uhlig, 'Condemn Cuban Officer, Tribunal Urges', *New York Times*, 28 June 1989.
18. Morganthau *et al.*, op. cit.
19. Borrell, op. cit.
20. 'Narcotics Agent Held in Boston on Drug Charge', *New York Times*, 16 Aug. 1989.
21. 'Thinking the Unthinkable', *Time*, 30 May 1988, pp. 12–19.
22. 'Should Drugs Be Legal? *Time*, 30 May 1988, pp. 36–8.
23. E. Marshall, 'Drug Wars: Legalization Gets a Hearing', *Science*, 241: 1157–9, 2 Sept. 1988.
24. 'Thinking the Unthinkable', op. cit.
25. Ibid.
26. Ibid.
27. J. F. Jekel and D. F. Allen, 'Trends in Drug Abuse in the Mid-1980s', *Yale Journal of Biology and Medicine* 60: 45–52 (1987).
28. A. Riding, 'Gangs in Colombia Feud Over Cocaine', *New York Times*, 22 Aug. 1988 (p. A1).
29. P. Kerr, 'Cocaine Glut Pulls New York Market into Drug Rings' Tug-of War', *New York Times*, 24 Aug 1988 (p. B1).
30. E. L. Englesman, 'Dutch Policy on the Management of Drug Related Problems', *British Journal of Addictions* 84: 211–18 (1989).
31. Ibid.
32. 'Arrests Skyrocketing As Drug Prices Tumble', *New Haven Register*, 13 Dec. 1988, p. 6.
33. 'Thinking the Unthinkable', op. cit.
34. 'Clog: Murder, Drug Cases Jamming State's Courtrooms', *New Haven Register*, 13 Dec. 1988 (p. 3)
35. G. James, 'Drug Arrests Are Crowding Local Prisons', *New York Times*, 12 Dec. 1988.
36. K. Johnson, 'Long Drug Sentences Run Into a Barrier', *New York Times*, 25 July, 1989.
37. J. C. Wilson, 'Against the Legalization of Drugs', *Commentary*, 89: 21–8, Feb. 1990.
38. T. Morganthau and M. Miller, 'Getting Tough on Cocaine', *Newsweek*, 28 Nov. 1988, (p. 76).
39. C. E. Johanson, 'Behavioral Studies of the Reinforcing Properties of Cocaine', National Institute on Drug Abuse Research Monograph 88: 107–24 (1988).

40. Engelsman, op. cit.
41. L. LoSciuto and M. A. Ausetts, 'Evaluation of a Drug Abuse Prevention Program: A Field Experiment', *Addictive Behaviors*, 13: 337–51 (1988).
42. P. Berger and J. Neuhaus, *To Empower People: The Role of Mediating Structures in Public Policy* (Washington DC: American Enterprise Institute, 1977).
43. C. Gorman, 'Crackdown on the Swiss Laundry', *Time*, 24 April 1989.
44. Ibid.
45. C. Dickey and R. Parry, 'A Drug Crackdown in the Alps', *Newsweek*, 10 April 1989.
46 Ibid.
47. J. F. Burns, 'Summit Calls for Anti-Drug Plan That Stresses Money Laundering', *New York Times*, 21 June 1988.
48. J. Castro, 'The Cash Cleaners', *Time*, 24 Oct. 1988.
49. Ibid.
50. 'U.N. Accord on Drugs is Signed', *New York Times*, 21 Dec. 1988.
51. M. Wines, 'US Says It Broke Vast Money Scheme', *New York Times*, 30 Mar. 1989.
52. *Time*, 28 Nov. 1988 (p. 76).
53. J. F. Jekel, D. F. Allen, *et al.*, 'Epidemic freebase cocaine abuse: case study from the Bahamas', *The Lancet* 1: 459–62, 1 March 1986.
54. L. Thompson, ' "Ice," new smokable form of speed', *Washington Post 'Health'*, 21 Nov. 1989, p. 11.
55. Kathleen Bishop, 'Fear Grows Over Effects of a New Smokable Drug', *New York Times*, 16 Sept. 1989, (p. 1).
56. Ibid.

Postscript

There is a danger of distorting the truth by focusing primarily on crack, as has been done in this book. This is crack's moment, but it probably will be superseded by 'ice' or some other drug within the next decade. Not that cocaine will disappear; it will be added to the growing panoply of psychoactive drugs that can be used, abused, and made and sold for profit. But the problem of crack cocaine must be seen in the context of the wider problem of substance abuse, and that, in turn, in terms of even broader problems of our current civilization. In western civilization, this means the problems of post-industrial society, where (to paraphrase Albert Einstein) we see a perfection of means and a confusion of ends.

Moynihan[1] and others[2] have argued that the current poverty and other problems seen increasingly in the USA, for example, as well as in other Western nations, come not as a residual of industrialism, when hands could still be trained to do useful work, but rather from the *post-industrial* world. In this, the present world, only a high level of intellectual-technical skills can enable one to escape unemployment and, eventually, the social scrap-heap. Those who, for whatever reason, are unable to obtain the education and skills needed by society face a bleak future.

Moynihan's particular point was that one cause of the persistence of poverty in the USA has been the decline of the family from the extended and nuclear family to what is increasingly becoming a norm, the *one-parent family*. This type of family is simply less able to cope economically and less able to give the child or children the support and stimulation they need for education and to fight the increasingly difficult challenges of modern life.

But Moynihan's bleak vision goes beyond the one-parent family to what is increasingly appearing, mostly due to the epidemics of acquired immune deficiency syndrome (AIDS) and crack cocaine: the *no parent family*! Whether it is the death of the mother from AIDS, or the abandonment of a child by a mother on crack, both of which are becoming increasingly common, the children of such families are in a terrible situation. Those children of AIDS mothers who are infected with the human immunodeficiency virus (HIV) are not only likely to die an early death, but it is also difficult to find foster homes for them, because people fear the AIDS virus. Likewise, children born to crack-addicted mothers may show major personality defects and may not be pleasant to care for, so it may be difficult to get foster homes for them as well. Moynihan predicts the growth of old-fashioned *orphanages* for these children, which suggests that somehow society is moving backward, rather than forward. His prediction is already coming to pass.[3]

There are in urban USA, as in many other countries, pockets of weakened families, inadequate education, poverty, teenage pregnancy, and high rates of AIDS and drug use, compounded by lack of purpose and hope on the part of the people themselves. It is difficult to blame the victims here, because even universities and governments lack the understanding and ability to respond adequately to the interlocked problems in these areas. The hopelessness of urban ghettos and barrios around the world is difficult to comprehend in its depth or extent. There is a deep spiritual vacuum which underlies and compounds the other difficulties and makes these populations breeding grounds for drug addiction.

At the other end of the economic spectrum, workers with good incomes still are stressed by the fast pace of post-industrial society and feel powerless to control the complex technical and economic systems they and others have created. Frequently suffering from an absence of deep commitments and values beyond the material and the present, they also seek relief in drugs, frequently in crack.

Traditional family, social, and religious values are often proclaimed to be out-of-date. Yet, looking at the plagues and poverty around us, we (the authors) believe that without a return to these values, the future of post-industrial society is bleak. Looking only at the cocaine crisis, the best bulwarks we have are strong families, strong and tightly knit neighborhoods, and deeply held personal values and commitments that transcend the material and the present moment. If quick profit and maximum pleasure are the predominant values of a society, it will be difficult to resist the scourge of crack cocaine now, and 'ice' and other drugs in the future.

These plagues can be conquered, but only by patterns of social living rooted in love and concern for the next generation and for other people in our own generation. Unless society has a perspective and value orientation that is rooted beyond the current world system, it will continue to treat an increasing proportion of its people as socially useless. Those who are cast off by society now have the power, through AIDS and drugs, whether purposely or inadvertently, to weaken society from within. What we need more than anything else at this time of crisis is a vision of hope, emanating from a meaningful faith and leading to renewal within ourselves and reorientation of our values.[4] According to Whitehead, 'To experience this faith is to know that in being ourselves, we are more than ourselves: to know that our experience, dim and fragmentary as it is, yet sounds the utmost depths of reality'.[5]

Paradoxical as it might appear, faith is the healing factor in the broken lives of many crack, cocaine, and coca paste addicts. Recognizing their powerlessness over the drug and a bankruptcy of their lives, they cry out in despair and yet in hope beyond themselves, to their therapists, and to the source of ultimate meaning of life. Their faith is expressed in a change of lifestyle, a re-creation of values, and a deeper sense of human community. We know pushers who no longer sell drugs; women destroyed by crack and prostitution turn around and live meaningful lives; and young men caught in the grip of crack and crime go straight and start life over. Perhaps this is what Immanuel Kant meant when he wrote that the critical analysis of human experience stresses the need for belief in God, freedom, and immortality.[6]

We believe that Siegel's suggestion – that the urge to use addictive drugs represents an inherent human drive like hunger, thirst, or sex – is incorrect. It is not a primary urge, but rather part of a desperate response to the tendency in modern society to reduce life to materialism, and to expect immediate gratification, or at least an easy escape from the threat of meaninglessness. To us, the problem of crack cocaine, among many others, shows the truth of the great statement of Augustine about AD 400 in the first canto of his *Confessions*: 'Thou has made us for Thyself, and our hearts are restless till they rest in Thee'.[7]

References

1. Daniel P. Moynihan, 'Toward a Post-Industrial Social Policy', *The Public Interest* 96: 16–27, Summer 1989.
2. Alvan Toffler, *The Third Wave* (New York: Bantam Books, 1980).

3. L. L. Creighton, 'The New Orphanages', *U.S. News and World Report*, 8 Oct. 1990, pp. 37–41.
4. Much of what follows was adapted from D. F. Allen, 'Epilogue: A Vision of Hope', in D. F. Allen, ed., *The Cocaine Crisis* (New York: Plenum Press, 1987), p. 223).
5. A. N. Whitehead, *Science and the Modern World* (New York: The Macmillan Company, 1962).
6. W. D. Geoghegan, from a Phi Beta Kappa invitation speech delivered in May, 1984, at Bowdoin College and reported in *The Key Reporter* vol. 49(4), Summer 1984.
7. *The Confessions of St. Augustine*, translated by F. J. Sheed (New York: Sheed & Ward, 1942), p. 3.

Appendixes

APPENDIX A : A GLOSSARY OF STREET DRUGS AND DRUG TERMS

Opiates

HEROIN ('Boy', 'Dope', 'Horse', 'Smack') – The most common injected narcotic drug. It causes severe physical withdrawal symptoms. Other narcotics are sometimes used, such as morphine, meperidine, percodan, codeine, etc.

MPPP – A synthetic heroin that is extremely potent by weight, which makes it especially dangerous because it is easy to inject overdoses. Moreover, if it is not made correctly, it will be contaminated with the extremely dangerous MPTP (q.v.).

MPTP – A byproduct in the manufacture of MPPP due to inadequate technique. It produces severe and irreversible Parkinson's Disease.

Depressants ('Downers')

METHAQUALONE ('Quaaludes', 'Ludes', 'Mandrax') – This is a sedative sometimes used for its psychic effects; can become habit forming, producing withdrawal symptoms.

BARBITURATES ('Barbs', 'Blue Devils', 'Red Devils', 'Yellow Jackets', 'Yellows') – The most commonly used barbiturates are Nembutals, Seconal, Amytal, and Tuinal.

TRANQUILIZERS – A number of these may be taken other than according to prescription: Equanil, Librium, Miltown, and, perhaps most commonly, Valium.

Stimulants ('Uppers')

COCAINE HYDROCHLORIDE ('Coke', 'Snow', 'Flake', 'White Lady', 'Lady' or 'White') – The best known stimulant, cocaine is most dangerous and addictive in its freebase form ('crack'). However, a significant percentage of cocaine powder snorters also become addicted.

CRACK ('Rock', 'White Cloud', 'Base') – The most common street name for freebase cocaine, probably called this because a crackling sound is made both when cocaine hydrochloride powder ('snow') is mixed with water and sodium bicarbonate to make the freebase cocaine, and when the crack is smoked.

METHAMPHETAMINE ('Speed', 'Crank') – a stimulant related to amphetamine that produces psychic effects similar to those of cocaine, because it also blocks dopamine re-uptake in the neural synapses. The drug causes paranoia.

ICE – A crystalline, smokable form of methamphetamine that produces a cocaine-like high and an unpleasant recovery. The high lasts for hours. It may soon rival crack in popularity in some places. 'Ice' is to methamphetamine what 'crack' is to powdered cocaine.

OTHER AMPHETAMINES – Different forms of amphetamine have been used, including Benzedrine, Biphetamine, and Dexedrine: the terms used include 'Speed', 'Black Beauties', 'Pep Pills', and 'Bumblebees'. See also the other products made from amphetamine, which follow.

MDMA – 3,4–methylenedioxy-methamphetamine ('Ecstasy').
At one time, ecstasy was thought to be safer than methamphetamine. Some psychotherapists have recommended using this drug as an aid to therapy, claiming that it lowers the psychic defenses of patients and increases their insight. Others disagree that it has any therapeutic benefit. In fact, long term, possibly irreversible, effects on the brain have been demonstrated; this apparently involves a severe reduction of serotonin levels.

MDE ('Eve') – Another modification of the basic amphetamine structure which is being studied to see if it should be made illegal. There are many other analogs being produced.

Hallucinogens

MARIJUANA ('Cannabis', 'Grass', 'Pot', 'Reefer', 'Weed') – This used to be considered safe by many, but it has been shown to produce psychosis, and research has shown there are long term negative effects on the brain and on human functioning from marijuana use. Hashish ('Hash') is closely related.

LYSERGIC ACID DIETHYLAMIDE ('LSD', 'Acid', or 'White Lightning'). The major hallucinogen of the late 1960s, LSD has unpredictable and sometimes horrifying effects on many users. Suicide has been reported during its use.

PCP (Phencyclidine [Phenyl-cyclohexyl-piperidine]) ('Angel Dust', 'boat', 'dust') – Related to an anesthetic agent, PCP causes mental aberrations, including hallucinations, delusions, and wild behavior. Deaths have resulted from its use.

Mixtures

SPACE BASING – A mixture of cocaine and phencyclidine (PCP, or 'Angel Dust'), which is called 'space basing'. This mixture may cause wild behavior and paranoia.

SPEEDBALLS – A mixture of a stimulant and an opiate , usually intravenous cocaine and heroin. The addicts think the upper and downer counteract the other's side effects, but in high doses both drugs depress the respiratory center. Very dangerous.

APPENDIX B : RULES FOR DRUG DEPENDENCE

These are taken from the *Diagnostic and Statistical Manual of Mental Disorders* (DSM–III–R). This is published by the American Psychiatric Association. The following are the diagnostic criteria for psychoactive substance dependence. These criteria apply to alcohol, opiates, cocaine, and other drugs.

A. At least three of the following:

1. Substance often taken in larger amounts or over a longer period than the person intended;
2. Persistent desire or one or more unsuccessful efforts to cut down or control substance use;
3. A great deal of time spent in activities necessary to get the substance (e.g., theft), taking the substance (e.g., chain smoking), or recovering from its effects;
4. Frequent intoxication or withdrawal symptoms when expected to fulfil major role obligations at work, school, or home (e.g.,

does not go to work because hung over, goes to work or school 'high,' intoxicated while taking care of his or her children), or when substance use is physically hazardous (e.g., drives when intoxicated);

5. Important social, occupational, or recreational activities given up or reduced because of substance use;

6. Continued substance use despite knowledge of having a persistent or recurrent social, psychological, or physical problem that is caused or exacerbated by the use of the substance (e.g., keeps using heroin despite family arguments about it, cocaine-induced depression, or having an ulcer made worse by drinking);

7. Marked tolerance: need for markedly increased amounts of the substance (i.e., at least a 50 per cent increase) in order to achieve intoxication or desired effect, or markedly diminished effect with continued use of the same amount.

8. Characteristic withdrawal symptoms (see specific withdrawal symptoms under *Psychoactive Substance induced Organic Mental Disorders*);

9. Substance often taken to relieve or avoid withdrawal symptoms.

NOTE: The last two items may not apply to cannabis, hallucinogens, or phyencyclidine (PCP).

B. Some symptoms of the disturbance have persisted for at least one month, or have occurred repeatedly over a longer period of time.

APPENDIX C : THE FOURTEEN BASIC STEPS TO RECOVERY

These are the steps used by Dr Nelson Clarke and his team in both inpatient and outpatient treatment of crack cocaine addiction in the Bahamas (Adapted from the Twelve Basic Steps of Alcoholics Anonymous).

Philosophy

Anyone who has had the misfortune to have become a habitual taker of drugs needs a framework of beliefs and facts which will help the individual to formulate strategies to break out of the drug-taking trap. The 'Fourteen basic steps to recovery' is a device designed to fill the above-stated purpose. The steps are not intended to be a magical formula by which an individual instantaneously becomes drug free. The steps are intended to aid those individuals who work with recovering drug users. The steps may be used as a tool for both individual and group work.

Steps

1. *Admit the Drug Problem*
Many persons who claim that they wish to stop using drugs are not fully aware of their problem's magnitude. Admitting the problems involves several processes. Individuals must first examine their lives while in a non-intoxicated state, reviewing the 'problem' and its overall effect on life in general. This step is perhaps the most difficult. For many drug users a 'crisis' of some sort (family, financial, etc.) may be the event that causes this self-examination to take place and afterwards the admission of the presence of the 'drug problem'. These processes may take quite some time to occur. For many individuals this is a very painful and humiliating event.

2. *Decision*
The single word 'decision' is the essence of the second step. After admitting the problem, the natural next event should be that the individual decides to do something about the problem – i.e., to stop using drugs immediately. Although this is a step that many drug takers will claim they have taken at some time or several times, many are unable to keep their decisions intact. For others even with good/sincere intentions, living up to the decision to cease using drugs is difficult if one tries to do so without help of some sort. The decision must be to stop using drugs, not to slow down. Slowing down never really works.

3. *Seek Help*
For those unable to cease using by solo effort, seeking help is necessary and vital. In some cases 'help' is poorly understood. Many individuals who seek help do not realize that they too have a large part to play in the process. It is not a passive process. Both the help seekers and help givers have important responsibilities in this process. Careful consideration must be given

to the roles and responsibilities on both sides. There must be honesty and openness on both sides. There must be reliability on both sides.

4. *Explore the Problem*

This is an ongoing process. Without continuous exploration and evaluation very little may be achieved, as each individual is different and may have different variations of a similar problem, which may demand varied solutions. Without exploration, a true appreciation of the individual's problem may never be achieved.

5. *Spiritual Awareness*

Man is composed of physical, mental and spiritual components. Spiritual beliefs may be valuable in helping the individual with a drug problem to overcome that problem. The acceptance of the existence of God, the Divine Jehovah, Allah, by whatever name he is called and the realization that this Power exists to aid the recovery process; the realization that this Power is available is a fact. However understanding the way in which this aid is accomplished may be difficult for many persons. Careful discussion and explanation is necessary for many individuals. Those who do not feel that they must do some work fall into the trap of saying 'I asked God to help me so I am cured of my drug problem,' or 'I have become a Christian so that's it, my drug problem has been solved'. These individuals may find that unless they make some personal effort that their problems remain.

6. *Self Control*

Self control, self discipline, is vital if one is to overcome the problem of habitual drug use/dependence. Controlling the physical self, the emotional self, the thoughts, and being able to exert control in the face of difficult situations is a must if recovery is to occur and be lasting.

7. *Make Future Plans*

Without plans for the future one may easily return to earlier behaviors and return to a lifestyle of drug usage.

Plans give purpose and meaning to the individual's future existence. Without plans anything may happen.

Plans may be immediate (daily plans), or long term (months, years). It is useless to make plans that are impossible, plans must be realistic.

8. Replacement Activities

Drug use may take over an individual's life to the extent that many long hours may be spent either in the search for drugs or actual use.

When one is attempting to change over lifestyle from drug using to non drug use (drug free lifestyle), it is vital that individuals consider what activities they may now become involved with. It must be remembered that the individual must go through the process of learning to enjoy normal healthy non drug related activities. This will take some time but if success is to be gained it must be done.

Some possible replacement activities include sports: e.g., soft ball, basket ball, table tennis, jogging, swimming.

Self improvement activities: e.g., upgrading one's education, learning a new skill – e.g., playing a musical instrument – a part time job, a new hobby.

Civic activities: i.e., joining a social club and becoming actively involved, volunteer work, becoming involved in community projects. Church related activities: young people's groups, church choirs, bible study groups, etc.

It must be remembered that one must have several different types of replacement activities if boredom is to be prevented. Also, some activities should be ones that can be carried out without involving other people, and should not depend to any great extent on external influences – i.e., the weather. Hence other useful replacement activities may include, reading, craft work, yoga, listening to music.

Additionally, replacement activities should not be financially burdensome.

9. Develop the Ability to Say 'No'

The drug taking person has become accustomed to saying yes when offered drugs. If the individual is to develop a drug free lifestyle, he/she must learn to say 'no' to drugs, not only when drugs are offered by others, but the individual must learn to say no to activities which may be drug-related. Whether the offer is made for the purpose of use or sale the answer must be no. Practice is important. Role play may help individuals to understand the process of saying no. One must say no with the mouth and the rest of the physical self. After saying no to drugs then one's behavior towards the individual offering the substance must be consistent with the words uttered. Leaving the situation immediately is always a good way of emphasizing the point.

10. *Avoiding Temptations*
Continued exposure to situations where drug use may occur is dangerous to the sobriety of the recovering drug addict. Therefore, avoiding persons who are drug users, and places where drug use occurs is essential.

One exercise which may help involves attempting to identify situations which may be tempting for each individual. People differ and therefore a situation which may be particularly tempting for one person may not be so for another person.

11. *Obtaining Support*
All individuals attempting to overcome their drug problems will find that support, or aid of some kind or another is helpful. Support may be moral, spiritual (religious), financial, emotional, therapeutic. Support may be obtained from a number of different systems. Support may come from the family, friends, peers (i.e., others who are also trying to overcome their own problems of drug dependence) from the church, from the community groups and many other avenues.

It is important that recovering drug addicts are able to identify their own support systems. Additionally the individual must clearly understand what responsibilities are involved if the support system is to be used effectively.

12. *Deal with Craving*
A craving is a severe desire or wish, in this instance the desire for drugs. Cravings may be extremely severe and may lead an individual back into the drug trap. A number of devices may be used to overcome and control cravings; physical exercise, relaxation and self-hypnosis are some methods that may be used.

Cravings may occur as persistent thoughts about drugs, or using drugs or past experiences of a pleasant nature associated with drugs. Reliving 'bad,' 'distasteful,' or painful past experiences associated with drug use may effectively counteract these mental cravings. Physical cravings may occur where the individual may experience bodily sensations commonly associated with drug use – i.e., symptoms/effects of the drug, or at times pains, aches in associated areas. These respond best to physical exercise and relaxation. Mood changes – i.e., changes in mood for no obvious reason, e.g. depression, elation, uneasiness – may occur. When identified as a craving these may respond to physical exercise, relaxation, or sometimes simply talking the matter over with an objective other person. Cravings may also occur in the form of dreams about drugs or drug use. The individual may awaken experiencing severe mental and physical cravings.

Important facts about cravings:
1. They cannot be conquered unless identified.
2. Once identified the individual must make a conscious effort to effectively overcome the craving.
3. The individual may experience craving of several types at the same time. This is common rather than extraordinary.
4. Cravings may be experienced up to 2 years after the last drug use.
5. Whatever happens in the way of cravings, the individual's resolve to remain drug free must be consistent.
6. It should always be remembered that if one holds out and does not respond to cravings – i.e., does not take drugs – the craving will go away eventually even if it takes several hours.

13. Repair Family Relationships

The drug user invariably damages the relationship between himself and his family. Repairing this relationship is important to the recovery process.

Admitting to the damages done by deceit, stealing and irresponsibility, and then making an effort to be open and honest with the family members, is important if the relationships are to be mended. Asking forgiveness is a necessary part of the process.

Making some attempt to compensate for the problems one has caused may help the process of repair.

It is unwise to expect immediate trust from family members and/or friends. Trust must be earned. It may take quite a while before doubts are removed from the family's mind. Consistent behavior, openness, and a willingness to share may help the process.

The recovering addict must remember that the onus is on him/her to initiate the repair process.

14. Helping Others Who Might Have the Problem

Often individuals who feel that they have achieved a measure of success in becoming drug free feel a deep desire to help others with the problem. They often become Messiahs, venturing into known drug areas and flaunting their success before ex-friends, who are still gripped in the drug trap. This is foolhardy and dangerous, and is not advised.

The ways to help others with the problem are:

1. Simply explaining to those who ask where help can be obtained.
2. Living as an example so that others may follow.
3. Joining a peer group – i.e., others who are making a visible and sincere effort to free themselves from the drug trap.

APPENDIX D : SOME INEXPENSIVE REFERENCE SOURCES
REGARDING DRUG ABUSE

Most of these sources, and many others, can be obtained by writing to the:

National Clearinghouse for Alcohol and Drug Information
P.O. Box 2345
Rockville, MD 20852

General

1. US Dept of Health and Human Service, Public Health Service, Alcohol, Drug Abuse, and Mental Health Administration. 'What You Can Do About Drug Use in America', 1988. DHHS Pub. No. (ADM) 88–1572.
2. US Dept of Health and Human Service, Public Health Service, Alcohol, Drug Abuse, and Mental Health Administration. 'Cocaine/Crack: The Big Lie', 1987. DHHS Pub. No. (ADM) 89–1427.
3. US Dept of Health and Human Service, Public Health Service, Alcohol, Drug Abuse, and Mental Health Administration. 'When Cocaine Affects Someone You Love', 1987. DHHS Pub. No. (ADM) 89–1559.

Schools

1. US Department of Education, 'What Works: Schools Without Drugs', 1989. Obtain at the above address or call, in the US, 1–800–624–0100.
2. US Dept. of Education, Office of Educational Research and Improvement, 'Drug Prevention Curricula', 1988.

The workplace

1. US Dept of Health and Human Service, Public Health Service, Alcohol, Drug Abuse, and Mental Health Administration. 'Workplace Drug Abuse Policy: Considerations and Experience in the Business Community', 1989. DHHS Pub. No. (ADM) 89–1610.

Community efforts

1. US Dept of Health and Human Service, Public Health Service, Alcohol, Drug Abuse, and Mental Health Administration. 'Drug-Free Communities: Turning Awareness into Action', 1989. DHHS Pub. No. (ADM)89–1562.
2. US Dept of Health and Human Service, Public Health Service, Alcohol, Drug Abuse, and Mental Health Administration. 'A Community Solution: Drug Abuse Treatment', 1989. DHHS Pub. No. (ADM) 89–1633.

Index